MONOLOGUES FOR SHOW-OFFS

Donna Daley & Julie Halston

Foreword by Brian O'Neil

HEINEMANN
Portsmouth, NH

Heinemann
361 Hanover Street
Portsmouth, NH 03801–3912
www.heinemanndrama.com

Offices and agents throughout the world

Performance rights information can be found on page 122.

CIP data is on file with the Library of Congress.
ISBN-13: 978-0-325-01227-8
ISBN-10: 0-325-01227-X

Editor: Cheryl Kimball
Production service: Melissa L. Inglis-Elliott
Production coordinator: Vicki Kasabian
Cover design: Joni Doherty Design
Authors' photograph: David Rodgers Photography
Typesetter: Tom Allen/Pear Graphic Design
Manufacturing: Steve Bernier

Printed in the United States of America on acid-free paper
12 11 10 09 08 VP 1 2 3 4 5

For Ralph and Anthony, with love.

Contents

MONOLOGUES FOR WOMEN

MONOLOGUES FOR MEN

What we do is called acting—be active!

—Richard Easton
Tony Award–winning actor

Foreword

I have seen hundreds—more likely thousands—of monologues over the years. What I like most about this collection is that there is never any doubt that the characters are involved in an active conversation—and a specific relationship—making the pieces alive and in-the-moment.

Julie and Donna write clever material. They have crafted monologues with built-in changes in pace and tone, always driving the action forward.

Even when dealing with serious or tender material, they have added touches of humor—always a plus—making the monologue more complex and surprising. And what is the one thing all casting directors want? To be surprised!

In addition, there is much valuable information from many notable professionals from all areas of the industry.

I really like this book. It is a welcome addition to the ever-expanding shelves of monologue books. It is both clear and concise—as well as gender-, age- and ethnic-friendly.

There is something for everyone.

So, go ahead—sink your teeth in and *show off*. You can't lose!

—BRIAN O'NEIL
AUTHOR OF *ACTING AS A BUSINESS: STRATEGIES FOR SUCCESS*

Preface

We are fortunate to know many talented actors, and we are aware of their constant search for fresh material. The pursuit of a perfect pair of contrasting monologues that quickly demonstrate an actor's talent and range seems never-ending. Well, here are some bold new selections for you.

Our friends helped us hone these monologues by allowing us to hear them in a variety of voices. We have divided the book by gender, but please don't let that limit you. For example, "The Korean Lesbian" was read by a thirty-year-old Caucasian man who related so strongly to the material that, by changing a few obvious specifics, he made it work for him. Any of the pieces can work well with any ethnic group. We were only specific in a couple of places where race is particular to the conflict itself.

We know you will add your own touch of genius, but in some of the monologues we have given you a little direction or a few tips, which can help them sail.

Throughout the book are also some bits of advice and amusing anecdotes from an array of show-biz professionals. These choice words from various perspectives are included to encourage you and to give you insight into the many aspects of the casting process.

The point of this book is to help you, the show-off, do just that. Surprise them. Surprise yourself. It's your moment. Knock 'em dead!

—DONNA & JULIE

Acknowledgments

Special thanks to the following people for their invaluable contributions to the making of this book: Lynn Ahrens, Carl Andress, Lisa Barnett, Walter Bobbie, Charles Busch, Dan Butler, Jim Carnahan, Jack Cummings III, Paul de Pasquale, Richard Easton, Kenneth Elliott, Starsky Eustache, Jesse Tyler Ferguson, Andrea Frierson, Anthony Gentile, Christopher Gentile, John Gentile, Jacob Harran, Richard Hester, Ralph Howard, Julian Ivey, Cheryl Kimball, John Kudan, Arven Liu, Margo Martindale, Adam McLaughlin, Elissa Myers, Eric Myers, Angela Newton, Michelle Ng, Brian O'Neil, Annie O'Sullivan, Matt Rockman, Jeff Sharp, Jared Smith, Susan Varon, and Lanette Ware-Bushfield.

Acknowledgments

When doing a monologue, you have to know who you are talking to. Be as specific as possible. If you are talking to one, you are talking to all.

—Margo Martindale
Actor

Advice

AFRICAN AMERICAN WOMAN

You know how I feel. I told you months ago to drop-kick his butt. Girl, you knew he wasn't free. Separated ain't divorced. Separated just means he can have his cake and change the frosting whenever he wants. Well, of course he's great in bed! He spends a lot of time doing it! Between you, his wife, and God-knows-who-else, he gets a lot of practice. He better be good! Oh, honey, they always make promises. By the time he leaves his wife, she'll be dead, and then he'll leave you for some bony-assed cheerleader. I'm stating the facts. And by the way, what he ever get you? A Prada bag? A Prada bag. Well, whoop-de-do! Chances are it's a knockoff, but even if it's real, you take a bag when it's got car keys in it and a diamond ring! Otherwise, it's just a bag to stash your heartache. You'll see. I ain't making this up. Even if—and it's a big if—he walks you down the aisle, you'll know he's a cheater. And a cheater doesn't stop cheatin'. He'll be making a date with a bridesmaid. You think you're crying now? Wait till you're married with two kids and he ain't home but half the time 'cos he's makin' time with some girl with her head in the clouds, just like you. She'll be crying. You'll be crying. The only one *not* crying is that loser. Don't you watch Oprah? Girl, you better start listening to your sisters. Kick his sorry ass to the curb! You need empowerment. You don't have no *real* man in your life. You got a part-time lover with a wife. Part-time, time to part. Honey, I'm your friend. I don't wanna see you hurt. He ain't boyfriend material. He's not husband material. He's not even good companion material. Why, my dog is a better companion! He's always happy to see me, and he pees outside. Now *that's* a good companion!

An Answered Prayer

WOMAN

Mr. Daniels, I understand perfectly why I am here. I welcome the opportunity to tell you my side of the story. I've been teaching sixth grade now for fifteen years. The day I became a nun was the happiest day of my life. I know this neighborhood very well. I grew up here. I was twelve years old when I started pulling my father out of bars. I vowed I would live a life of service, surrounded by people who aspired to do better. And I found it at Holy Cross. I keep in touch with many of my former students. I know we've made a big difference in many of these girls' lives. I first saw Carlos about two years ago in the playground one afternoon. I asked him what he was doing there, and he said he was the brother of Maria Rivera. Well, of course I knew he was lying, since I knew all my students' families. I told him to get off our property or I would call the police. He left, but over the next few months I'd see him—up the block or across at the library. He was always hanging around. Almost overnight, I noticed a real change in many of the girls. They were constantly fighting with each other, with us, out sick all the time, not doing their work. Some of my best students were suddenly . . . uncontrollable. Finally, Maria's sister told me that Maria was on drugs. Crack. She said a lot of the girls were doing it, and Sugar Man was giving it to them. I went to the precinct. They told me Carlos was Sugar Man and it was known around he was a big crack dealer. They just couldn't arrest him till they caught him in the act. I watched Carlos numerous times plying his trade. I'd call the police. No one did anything. Nothing. Then I realized they were not going to do anything. I have never see this place so torn apart. I prayed and prayed and prayed, and one day I got an answer. There were no voices in my head, no music. It was just a feeling—a feeling of extreme peace. I knew the Lord was giving me a sign of grace. You know, Mr. Daniels, being a nun is seen as a limited life, but wearing this habit freed me in a way that I have never truly understood until that moment. I confronted Carlos.

He said he welcomed the opportunity to talk with me, since so many of my students were his friends. He was so cocksure of himself. "Go ahead, Sister. You live such a miserable life. Have some fun for once in your life." And he just laughed and laughed. And that's when I shot him, Mr. Daniels. I shot him three times. Three times. People think I did it because I went crazy. They say it must be a mistake, that I was defending myself. It was no mistake. I was doing what the Lord wanted me to do. So you see, Mr. Daniels, whatever happens with this trial is fine with me. I'm not afraid.

An Appreciation

WOMAN

Thank God he's asleep. I'm so tired I can't even talk about how tired I am. This is something. You understand, Ma, that now that you've come over you will not be allowed to go home. Because when Jim comes home tonight and actually expects to eat, I will not be getting out of this chair. I may never get out of this chair. Unless you cook it, Mom, there will be no dinner in this household tonight. How did you ever do it? And with four of us yet? Jesus. He cried for hours last night. I felt terrible for him, but I just didn't know what to do. I tried rocking. I tried playing. I tried feeding. I was so desperate I even started singing. Well, then he really started to howl. Mom, now that I've had a baby, I have to say I'm in awe. For one thing, you always kept the house so clean and neat, and I remember dinner was always six o'clock sharp. How the hell did you do it? I mean, it's not like you had any help. I ended up doing the laundry the other night at one-thirty in the morning. You never did laundry in the middle of the night. And—I just remembered this—you used to fold our clothes in our drawers like it was in a store or something. I can barely find the time to just shove everything in. How did you do it? Are you kidding? Really? Coffee, cigarettes, and diet pills. Really. Well, it makes sense. It was a different era. Of course, I don't think those things are going to come back into fashion any time soon, but, man, it must have made things a lot easier. You know, I do remember after Kathy was born you got your figure back pretty quickly, and now I know why—coffee, cigarettes, and diet pills. Wow, this is something to know. Leave it to me to have a baby during an era of good health and natural well-being. But, Mom, did you ever get depressed or feel overwhelmed? Let's face it, Ma. We were a rowdy bunch. No, huh? You enjoyed it all. I mean, along with the coffee, cigarettes, and diet pills, you loved being a mom, didn't you? You never felt like you had to be anything else. God, that sounds so nice. I'm already worrying about the end of my maternity benefits. You didn't get so anxious like I do. You accepted things. Maybe that's why you were such a good mom. Thank God you're here. No, no, sit. I'm gonna make the coffee.

The Audition

WOMAN

I am so sorry to be late. I forgot to get my parking ticket validated from my last appointment, and so I either had to pay twenty dollars or go back and get it validated. It's kinda crazy here, with all the cars and all. Oh, yes, let me take my sunglasses off. It's very sunny here. Not here per se. I mean L.A. in general. My agents thought I should meet you. A lot of theatre and some films—film. It was a lot of fun. *Die Hard Five: The Final Apocalypse.* Bruce Willis was a doll. My headshot is about two years old. Maybe three. Or five. No more than that. I plan on getting new headshots while I'm out here. I'm staying with a friend in Burbank. Everyone is very friendly here. I haven't booked anything yet per se, but I'm getting close, according to the feedback I'm getting. I mean, not every movie or TV show can be about kids, right? Well, maybe it can, but I think I'll book something very soon. What I do best is the sort of wry friend or take-charge kinda gal. I don't know if I mentioned that I've received a number of awards for my work in Chicago and New York. Chicago has very intense weather, yes. I have done a lot of musicals. I'm a big belter. The tours I've done have never come through L.A. per se, but I've been to Sacramento, so I am familiar with California. I know this is a general, so I didn't read a script or anything, but I was wondering about the female roles in the film. Of course, I know I'm not right for the lead, but I'm wondering about the second or even third lead. Oh, there is only one principal female role in the whole film? Oh, I didn't know. Well, cameo roles are great. Sometimes they are the best ones. They can really pop. Of course, stars would want to do them—lots of fun. So . . . I'm so glad I met you both. I hope the movie is a big hit, and, if you're looking for the wry friend, keep me in mind. I'm around. Oh, can I get my ticket validated from here? Oh, there's no validation here? At the desk on the way out. Well, thank you. Thank you again. (*She takes her sunglasses out again and, with as much dignity as she can muster, goes out the door.*)

I think the key thing to remember when going in to audition for anything, is to do your best to just be yourself. It sounds trite, but it's ultimately all that you have. Sure, you've got your high notes, your amazing kicks, and your killer acting chops, but those things don't add up to much without the charm and glow of your own inner fire.

—CARL ANDRESS
DIRECTOR/AUTHOR

Awakening

WOMAN

It was luck, pure luck. Someone just grabbed me and pulled me over a fence. My chest was burning. There was a lot of dirt in my mouth. I ran up a hill. Honestly, it was all so quick, so sudden. I wasn't thinking. I thought he was right behind me. There was a lot of noise—people screaming, crashing sounds. I remember seeing a lot of chairs. I could hardly breathe. I fell on the ground and woke up in a hospital. If you've ever been to Thailand, you know how serene and peaceful those beaches are, but that morning . . . Well, you saw the pictures on TV. It was much worse than even that. We were having breakfast and, believe it or not, my husband had just said what a glorious day it was and . . . and a second later we scrambled for our lives and he was swallowed. Y'know, the irony is that Dave was an excellent swimmer and I can barely float, but I managed to survive a catastrophic tsunami. I had a concussion and a few broken ribs. Time stopped. I don't remember much. Somehow I got back to America and we had a memorial service for my husband even though we didn't have my husband. I'm a writer by profession, but for the first time in my life I was at a loss for words. My mind became a windshield wiper battling a heavy rain. It was hard to look ahead, so I drove my life in the slow lane. Autopilot. It was hard to get anything done. My sister in frustration called a locksmith for me because apparently my back door was broken for months. He came one late afternoon. He worked quickly and quietly. I recognized that he was Thai. It's not everyday you encounter a Thai locksmith in Connecticut, so I asked him how he came to be in New London. He didn't answer for some time, but when he spoke his English was very good. Almost in a whisper, he told me the tsunami wiped out his family—his wife, his daughter, his son. He was living with his cousin. He pulled a picture from his shirt. His children were beautiful. The wave caught me again, but this time I was on terra firma. Words just rushed out of me. I couldn't stop them. I was suddenly feverish as the thoughts and words spilled out. How I knew. How terribly, terribly, terribly sorry I was, but that I knew, I really knew . . . the panic and loss and fear. I showed him a picture of my husband. Showed him my scars. Tumbling, tumbling the words came out. My hands were shaking. He was crying. We just held each other. We held each other a long time in my kitchen. We put our foreheads together and felt each other's breath. Finally, we parted. He bowed his head and left. My neck was suddenly cold from the October chill, but somehow it felt lovely and warm. And even through the gray twilight, I could see so clearly across the pond. The birch trees were silver, bright and sharp. I remembered the taste of mango and orange. I never saw him again but often think of him. I started a fire and took pen to paper, and the words just flowed.

Baby Charlie

YOUNG WOMAN

I'm not going to hurt him. I just want to see my baby, please. If you don't mind. Look, he's right over there. Just for a minute. I won't even pick him up, I promise. I shouldn't have done what I did. And I didn't mean to leave him there like that. I know that now. He'll probably be fine, right? Just let me look at him sleep, please? Then you can throw me out, and I won't try again. I won't. I won't. Thank you. People think I'm so bad for him, you know. But they don't know everything. I got all scrambled up with all the moving going on inside me. I was all shaky. Everything was all, like, mixed up and so loud. But look at him there all quiet. How can he be so little? Don't let him fool you. He's tough. I got the scars to prove it. He was banging the crap out of me for, like, two days. My body was all banging, and the banging in my head. I didn't even know I was running or I was ripping up. All these people told me about the blood after. I didn't even see it. There was too much inside and outside of me everywhere. I was so messed up and kind of freezing and freaked. It was crazy. I shouldn't have left him there in the snow. I know I shouldn't have left him there. I know, but I didn't know that then. Why doesn't everybody shut up about that? He's okay, isn't he? I'm telling you, he's a ballbuster. Look at his eyes all sleeping. He dreams so nice and soft. He looks like he's plastic. I gave him a name already. I hope he keeps it. His name is Charlie. I had an Uncle Charlie. He was nice. His actual name wasn't really Charlie. Everyone just called him that. His name was really Cuffbert. I could name him Cuffbert, but I've probably screwed him up enough already, so I'll leave it at Charlie. And it sounds classy, kind of. Right? Like a Prince or something? Hold on. I just need one more second. One more. Okay, I'm ready. Can you smoke in here? Okay, I'm leaving. Bye, Charlie.

The Barfly Philosopher

WOMAN

Let me ask you something, Janey. And I ask you because we are sittin' in this bar and I've already had a few and I'm feeling feisty. Lemme ask you, is all life valuable? Like, if someone is really smart and influential and doing good things all over the place. Isn't he—or she, I know, I know—more valuable than some crack addict who is just gonna die on the street anyway? I'm just asking—posing the question, you know. Sometimes when I see these scumbags who are on the earth, I think getting rid of them would be a service to the world. Janey, I'm not trying to play God. Are we gonna talk God here? 'Cause that's a whole 'nother discussion. No, I'm just saying is one person more valuable than another. Like that game we used to play. If you're stranded on a desert island, which foods would you bring with you? So if there's room for only so many people on the planet, which people would you bring? And we know there's not enough room on the planet and all the resources are being used up. We know that, Janey. See, I was just thinking that maybe, just maybe, we should take stock of who should stay and who should go. It's not ethnic cleansing. It's everybody cleansing. (*To bartender*) I'll have another. Any vodka is fine. See, if I was in power, I would make all citizens take a test. The test would take into account lots of things: intelligence, motor skills, speciality skills, emotional intelligence, and overall attractiveness. If you don't pass, you have a year to pull yourself up, and, if you still fail after that, you're done. Lethal injection. *Or*, if you're a hardened criminal who won't or can't reform, you're toast, too. *Or*, if you're two drunk chicks sitting in a bar three times a week, you're done, too! (*Laughs explosively*) Janey, I'm kidding. I'm kidding. What the—of course I was joking. I didn't mean to offend you. Janey, I'm drunk, for Chrissakes! And hey, newsflash: so are you, Janey. Tommy, another round. Enough with the "deep conversation!"

Both of Us

WOMAN

"I am only human." This is what you say to me? This is your explanation? What kind of an excuse is that? "I am only human." What are the rest of us? Gods? Animals? Muffins? You screwed up. But, please, own up to it. Please. Just once, okay? Just once don't blame it on something or someone else. We have all been given the same set of rules, here. We all have needs, drives, desires. We—all of us "only humans"—have to strive to keep these impulses under control—or in our pants, in this case. We "only human" people also come equipped with a moral barometer and a free will. We took a vow. A vow, remember that? In sickness and in health, for better or worse? Well, was she better or worse? It doesn't matter. It isn't about her. It's about us. Us together. Our life, our bond. I have believed in this so strongly, and I believed that you did, too. But now I don't even know what it is I believe or should believe. You know, what is undoing me the most isn't that you trashed my trust. It really isn't. It's that you're cocky about it. You somehow think you have a right to betray me. I'm having some difficulty with that, not just with you but with myself. I can't do it. I try to convince myself that I can, but I can't do it. I can't go through with it—you know, the "death-do-us-part" part. It is a promise I can't keep. I can't stay with you 'til the end, because I can't forgive you—not for being "only human" but for not being a man about it. And I can't find it in myself to live with that about you, which makes me disappointed in the both of us. I guess you could say I'm "only human," too.

The Breakup

YOUNG WOMAN

Well, I just told him, "Oh no. Oh no. You are *not* breaking up with me. No way." I mean really. He comes to me and has the nerve to tell me he's seeing this other girl, which of course means he's sleeping with this other girl, and maybe we should break up because he's become *attached* to her, and he thinks it's not fair to me and this is the right thing to do. Well, first of all, what does he mean *attached* to her? Like what? Like a clasp on a bracelet? He didn't say he loved her. He didn't say he was attracted to her. He said he was attached to her. Then he tells me in that phony-baloney way, "Oh, it's not fair to you." Yeah, right. Oh—and it's the right thing to do. The right thing to do is not be a creep who sleeps around on the girl you're dating. I have the right to break up with him, not the other way around. It's my prerogative. Can you believe this? I do the breaking up here. *I'm* the victim. Right? And I told him, "You were the one who wanted to go out with me so much." I wasn't even that interested when we started going out, remember? Remember I called you and said, "This guy is—eh, nothing special," remember? I did. I called you. You just don't remember, but I remember. He pursued me, and I thought, "Well, y'know, he's a nice guy. He's cute." I gave him a chance, and look where it got me—dumped for some slut. Well excuse me, I do the dumping here! I want it known that I broke off with him because he's a two-timing creep. What do you mean maybe he's in love with her? Are you out of your mind? He can't be in love with her. He's a cheater. Cheaters don't love. They just cheat. Trust me, I know. There are not two sides to every story. Sometimes there is, but not this time. There is only one side to this story, and it is that I have been victimized and violated and I hope he gets herpes of the face and falls off a bridge. What? No, I just had the burger and the salad—no fries. I gotta get back to the office. Well, I'm glad you agree. I just had to dump him.

Dress well. Dress simply. Don't come dressed as the character, although suggesting some of the character is great. If you wear something simple that fits you, we will spend your audition looking at your performance.

Always hold onto the sides, even if you have the scene memorized. If you try to do the scene or monologue from memory, your audition becomes about watching an actor try to remember the lines and not about the actor acting. If you are hired, then you can memorize them. It makes people on the other side of the table very nervous when people stand up there without holding onto the sides.

Don't chew gum. Ever.

Don't lie. If you are right out of college and have no professional credits, then just list your college credits on your resume. They want to know what you have actually done. People get their Equity Cards on Broadway shows all the time.

See the show you are auditioning for. If you can't do that, read the script or listen to the CD. Find out as much about it as you can.

It is so much harder on your side of the table than it is on ours. We are both waiting for that moment when you come into the room and you are exactly who we are looking for. There's nothing better, and it almost makes up for all the rest of it!

—RICHARD HESTER
PRODUCTION SUPERVISOR
JERSEY BOYS

Cable Lady

WOMAN

I love cable, especially on sweaters. I like it. I like to knit. I like to purl, drop one, pick up, drop three. It's a pattern that holds up—timeless. You can run it through anything. Great on socks. I do it to relax, mostly—a kind of meditation. It started as a hobby, but then it just took off. I don't really care about what I'm making. It's the process that I enjoy. I can make a sweater for everything. Nothing is too large or too small. I don't know what is so special about it—mine, I mean. A lot of people do it. There are knitting circles everywhere—clubs, organizations, foundations. It's the new wave of culture. What people are realizing is you can make anything out of yarn. If it can't be made out of yarn, it can be covered in it. And it brings people together. Everything in the world worth having should have a cozy—a cover—to protect it, to keep it from harm. I wish there was an international "Knit-Your-Way-to-Peace Day." Wouldn't that be lovely? To have all nations drop their guns—for one afternoon—and knit. Just pick up some knitting needles instead. Make some cozies for their firearms. This is a scud missile cozy I have here. I got the dimensions from the Internet. Sometimes I think you people come in with all your cameras because you think I'm a little wacky, idealistic, eccentric fool who likes to waste time doing arts and crafts. But, I'm actually a warrior. A needlework radical. My little sticks here are my weapons of love. They keep moving to the buffer zone, and I knit for world peace—one stitch at a time. If I have to cover the whole world with my yarn, I will protect it—the planet—from itself. It will be safe and warm. In its cabled cozy. A kind of global warming. Because that's what we need, don't you think?

Cleansing

YOUNG WOMAN

For the billionth time, I'm not starving myself. God! I'm not trying to lose weight. Why would I do that? Do you think I'm fat? You must think I'm fat. You do. You think I'm fat. Just say it, then. Otherwise, why do you think I'm trying to lose weight, if you don't think I'm fat? Seriously, why do you think I am on a diet, then? If you say that I am on a diet one more time, I am never going to eat again, I swear. Go ahead, say it. Go ahead, say it. Go ahead, say it. For the last time, I'm not on a diet—hear me—a diet. Only fat people diet. I'm on a fast. Like a monk. It is done to achieve balance and enlightenment. A fast is sacred and spiritual. That's why monks fast. It isn't something you do to lose weight. The weight loss is just a bonus. It is something your body decides, not you. You have to trust your body's decision. It's not dangerous. It's healthy. If you don't believe me, go ask a monk. The formula contains everything a person needs for nutrition and stamina. Everything. Cabbage water, cayenne pepper, and coke syrup is so enough for anyone to live on—for probably ever. Rids you of toxins. It's a fact. It isn't weird or trendy. It is backed up by scientific evidence and movie stars the world over. I have only done it for ten days, and already I feel cleansed and calm and pure. So bug off, okay? Leave me alone! You should try it. You have so much toxic build-up, you don't even know. You and Dad are, like, so into food. It's all you think about morning, noon, and night. First thing in the morning, what do you have? Breakfast. Then lunch, then dinner. Then another day—breakfast, lunch, dinner, all over again, and again, day after day. See what I mean? Can't you feel it, everything putrefying? Of course you can't. You are blinded by all your poisons. I can hear it in your voices. The way you talk in clogged tones. And what you say—listen to yourselves. You say things like people don't have enough meat on their bones. Eeeewww! You carnivores are so obsessed with meat. What does that say about you? That is so disgusting. Well, don't worry. You have plenty of meat on your bones—eww, wait a minute. That image is, like, seriously making me puke. I got to go. I am not doing it on purpose, not this time. It is you. This conversation is toxic, and you people are making me heave. You're worried about me? How sad. What a joke. So sad it makes me laugh, really. Like, so laughable I want to cry. I can't decide which. But I know I've totally got to chuck. Ooooh, why can't you be normal parents?!

The Color of Love

AFRICAN AMERICAN WOMAN

Just because she's dating this guy doesn't mean she hates being African American. Susan, you're overreacting. Keisha's not betraying her race, for God's sake. She might actually be in love. I think *you're* being a racist. You know what? Maybe we shouldn't have this conversation. You're my colleague and my mentor, and I respect you, but I just don't agree with you on this subject. Well, I *do* know a little bit about this because . . . the love of my life was white. College. SMU. All four years, I had a boyfriend. Me and Jared. We were mad for each other. We both loved classical music, we both loved cooking, we both loved the color orange, we both loved Halloween. In fact, one year we went as a black-and-white cookie. We were just very in sync. It was amazing. Our parents were a little taken aback at first, but eventually it became a non-issue. Then, right before graduation, something happened to me. These voices in my head kept saying, "Okay, school is ending, and now get on with the real world." The real world, where black is black and white is white. I guess I just freaked. I brought it up to Jared. He was like, "Don't be ridiculous. We're madly in love. We'll move to New York, get married, I'll be the big lawyer, you'll be the big broadcaster, and that's it. End of story." End of story. I couldn't wrap my mind around things. No white-shoe law firm would want Jared to have a black wife, and no self-respecting, empowered sister is going to marry a white man. And what about our kids? Black? White? In between? It was all too complicated. I felt like I was betraying my ancestors if I married Jared. My heritage was stronger than my heart. Just like what you want Keisha to do. I couldn't just love Jared, even though no one made me happier than he did. I broke it off. He was devastated. We both cried in the front seat of my car. He went off to law school. Obviously, I stayed here in D.C. And you know, Susan, I did make my family and friends proud, being a successful anchor and local celebrity, but guess what? I lost something as well. You want to hear the ultimate joke?

Just the other day, my mother said to me, "I wish you could find a nice guy like Jared. Your father and I always liked him." Susan, I lost the love of my life. I heard through a friend in New York that Jared got married to a Brazilian girl and now they're expecting. I'm sure they'll have a beautiful baby. You know I date from time to time. Hell, you've set me up a few times. And what do I always say? I'm never attracted. Susan, I'm begging you to let Keisha date whoever she wants. Let her decide. Because I'm telling you, love is love, and it comes in many colors. All these years later, I still love Jared. And I just can't get over him.

The key to a good audition is for the actors to try, against all odds, to present themselves as who they are, not who they think we want them to be. It's such an unnatural place, the audition room, that the more natural ease an actor can muster, the more likely they are to impress the people on the other side of the table. It's hard for actors to remember (or, in fact, to believe), but we are as desperate to like them as they are desperate to be liked.

—JIM CARNAHAN
CASTING DIRECTOR

Curtis

AFRICAN AMERICAN WOMAN

I lost the use of my legs two years ago August nineteenth. I got shot in the spine. The man who shot me—Mr. Mitchell is his name—shot me here, right here, in the end of my back. Between the L-3 and L-4, to be exact. I was in my hallway. It was in the afternoon, around four o'clock. I was with my two kids—Curtis, my twelve-year-old, and Theresa, my baby. I just picked up Theresa from daycare. She was two. And she was carrying on because she wanted Curtis' gummi bears. I'd had a long day, and Curtis wasn't helping any. He had his headset on over his ears and was teasing Theresa with the gummi bears. I yelled at Curtis to help me and not to be such an agitator. Next thing I know, there's this noise, and then there is no sound at all. I'm lying on the tiles—on the floor—and I'm feeling all this wet under me, and it's all blurry, and all these people are around me, and I hear sirens, and Theresa and Curtis are screaming "Mommy," and there's this man—Mr. Mitchell—middle-aged white man, a nervous-looking thing, hunched over me, talking to me real close to my face, like we're friends. He said he was my new neighbor. He said he was sorry. He just moved in down the hall. He never meant to hurt me, he says. He was trying to protect me, he was saying. He thought that Curtis had a gun. He never meant to shoot me. He meant to shoot Curtis. He meant to shoot my Curtis because he thought Curtis was attacking me or something. I'm thinking, "Thanks, sir, but looks like *you* got the gun." This is what he's going on about. He wants me to thank him for protecting me while I'm bleeding to death on the floor. They just about had to pry that Good Samaritan off of me to arrest him. We can all feel so much safer now, can't we? Praise be to Mr. Mitchell, a man so willing to come to the aid of a woman in distress. This is how it went down in the court. Somehow he got off on some kind of self-defense claim—an appropriate response he had to a potentially dangerous situation. Any situation is potentially dangerous when you're carrying a loaded gun, don't you think? There is some kind of hole in the logic here that went unnoticed. According to Mr. Mitchell, I think I was supposed to thank him for his neighborly assistance, even if it was shamefully misguided. What would I have done without him? What would we all do without the chivalrous Mr. Mitchell and others like him? They treated him like some kind of hero for protecting me—or attempting to protect me. I can't say that I am not angry. I am. But, in my own way, I'm grateful to Mr. Mitchell. Truly grateful. Seriously grateful. Because if he was the great marksman he thought he was, my boy, Curtis, would be the owner of this nifty chair I'm sitting in. And I can tell you, as sure as I'm sitting here, Mr. Mitchell would be one sorry dead man. Because I would have killed a man in cold blood, which I wouldn't deny or sugarcoat. And something tells me I would, no doubt, be in prison for a mighty long time. That would be how the story goes instead of how it is. Sometimes things, as bad as they seem, might work out for the better. So, thank you, Mr. Mitchell. I thank you. I thank you from the bottom of my L-3/L-4.

A Dancer

WOMAN

Barney, stop crying. This is crazy. I'm a dancer. What is the big deal? That's a good thing. I'm a very highly trained, professional dancer. I take my clothes off, but so what? Of course men look at me up there. That's the point, isn't it, Barney? I don't care about any of those jerks. It's just a job, and there isn't a whole lot out there to get all choosy about. It's not like I have any other skills to offer, you know? I was so relieved to find out I had a talent. Not for dancing. For nudity. I'm good at it, I guess. They pay me money for it. You don't know what it's like being on your own at sixteen. You got to go to soccer games and proms. Your family probably ate together every night, had salads and dinner conversations with napkins. You can try to hide it, Barney, but I've heard you say "please pass the salt" on a number of occasions. That's a dead giveaway. I'm just saying. It would be nice if I came from a fancy family. It would be nice *if* a lot of things. It would be nice if the streets were paved with candy corn and dogs could talk and we all pooped Pop Tarts. But you've got to make the best of what you've got, don't you? So wipe your nose, and let's be thankful for every fool who wants to watch me slide bare-ass down a pole. I don't know what the fascination is, but who are we to question it? I say hooray for them. Amen. Now would you please pass the salt?

I first auditioned for The Lion King *when I was eight and continued to audition for three years. I learned something important—don't give up! I had so many callbacks for Simba that, by the time I got the role, the dance routine was in my bones.*

—Julian Ivey
Eleven Years Old
Actor, Simba on Broadway

Do as Mama Say

AFRICAN AMERICAN WOMAN

Suggestion: Try a Caribbean accent.

I need a three-pound fowl. Got that? Not a two, not a four. Two is too scrawny; four too fatty. You get going. You hear me, girl? And don't go wandering around talking to all everybody about nonsense. Smiling at all those boys. They got nothing else to do but talk at your face while they're putting their stuff up your skirt—without you even knowing it. You start answering all the questions, you'll end up coming home with more in your panties than you left with, and soon it'll grow into something else. I'm saying to you, it's as easy as that. Now get. I need a three-pound fowl. You pick it out and have him kill it right then and there. I'll know if he don't kill it fresh in front of you, cuz you gonna make him give you the feet and the head in a separate brown paper sack. You get the whole chickapoo—you listening?—not just the innards and the throat. And if I see that those feet don't fit with that body or the head is a two-pound head, not a three-pound head, your head will fit just fine. You hear me, girl? Get going. But change that dress you got on. It matches the color of your skin. You look naked on the street standin' up. Is that what you want? You want them to think that? You better not. Get going, now. Hurry back. I got enough to worry about, and I can't wait all day. I'm hungry as a fox waiting for those chickens. Now scat, girl.

The Doyenne of Boca

MATURE WOMAN

Shirl, you'll love it! Boca is the best! Alright, alright, I promise no hard sell, but can I just say one small thing? One small thing as you sit and sip your Starbucks Iced Coffee Mocha from Boca, which we have on just about every third corner, so it is just like New York. Look around. There's so much to love. The water—beautiful. I never go in, but it's there. The weather—beautiful. We're indoors most of the time, but you look out and it's there. The shopping—ah! Beautiful. We've got Bloomies, Neiman's, Nordstrom's. I never go—they're too pricey—but they're there. You see what I'm saying? It's all here, Shirl. You want golf? Three courses within a ten-mile radius. I've never gone, but friends tell me they are absolutely beautiful. Tiger Woods is down here sometimes. Oh, and darling, they've just opened a brand new Arts Center downtown. Theatre, music, whatever you like—it's there. I haven't been, but the pictures in the paper—beautiful! They're even starting a series, "Broadway Goes Boca," where the Broadway stars come down here to perform. We'll look into it because I love that Patti LuPone. I'm telling you, Shirl, Boca has it all! And darling, there's a synagogue right near us. Beautiful. We never go, but it's there. So you see, Shirl, Boca is very metropolitan. It's one of the reasons we decided we could retire here. Well, most of the time Arthur and I play bridge. In the activities room. It's beautiful, and it's right downstairs. And you'll never believe who we partner with! Miriam and Lester Sussman! Yes, I know, I know. I never liked them much when we all lived in Scarsdale, but you know what? They play a beautiful game of bridge, and they're here, Shirl. They're here!

The Elitist

MATURE WOMAN

My daughter says that I'm an elitist. An elitist. I said to her, "Since when does having impeccable manners and well-made clothes mean you're an elitist?" She just shakes her head and says, "Oh, Mother, face it—you are a snob." Well so be it. I'm sorry. It pains me to see the kind of behavior that passes for acceptable these days. Email? Good God! The Death of Polite Society. I know a woman who was recently widowed, and people emailed her condolences! Atrocious! If you can't take the time to sit down and write out a proper card, then don't call yourself a friend. Am I wrong? I don't think so. Is it snobby to expect people to say "please" and "thank you" and "you're welcome" and speak in full sentences instead of grunts and groans? I don't think so. And why is everyone so overweight these days? What happened to a little restraint, a little self-control? There is no proper order to anything anymore, and it makes me so tired. I see my daughter and my son-in-law racing around like chickens without their heads, keeping up their careers, their house, their kids—all because they want to "do it all themselves." It's ridiculous. I told my daughter to get a full-time nanny and housekeeper, but she said no. No, they have a lovely part-time baby-sitter who helps her clean sometimes. Part-time? Well, I'm sorry to say that part-time frequently means half-baked. If you want to do something, you have to do it right—one hundred percent commitment. I was a full-time wife and mother and good God that was enough! I had a full-service staff. I never cooked a meal or cleaned a dish, but I made sure my children were properly clothed and fed. They went to great doctors and had wonderful schooling. They had lovely friends and marvelous experiences. Is that elitist or just lucky? And I stayed married to the same man for forty years. Was it heaven on earth? Of course not, but there you are. My husband died peacefully and his two children came out healthy, smart, and rich. I'm not an elitist, just a realist. I might have had everything, but I sacrificed a lot. There you are.

Email

WOMAN

Joanne, I'm sorry I didn't get back to you right away, but I have a reason. I'm avoiding someone. Oh, this is so dumb I can hardly stand it, but I was stupid enough to answer an email from an old childhood acquaintance. Well, to be honest, someone I actually hated. "Hey, Lisa, is this you? I'm so glad I found you!" That was in the subject column, so I opened it. First mistake. It's Eleanor Spofford. Yeah, Spofford, like the detention center. Eleanor Spofford was kicked out of our grammar school for carrying a knife in her prayer book. She was suspended from high school three times, one time for clocking the music teacher over the head with a clarinet. She constantly bullied me. She stole everything from me: hats, pencils, books. Once she threw my rain boots down the compactor shoot. Am I painting a clear picture? So I open the "I'm-so-glad-I-found-you" email, and I get this three-page letter with every detail of her life for the last hundred years: her divorce, her kids, what her house looks like, what she's interested in, that she's an Aquarius. Oh, and get this. Her email address is spoff666. Six six six! Why would I even consider writing back to someone with that address!? What was I thinking!? Well, now I hear from spoff666 every day. First, she'd send articles. Then it was jokes. Then it was photos, tons of photos. Then it was links, links to other links and then to blogs, including her blog. Oh, yes, spoff666 has her own blog. And if I don't respond to spoff666 within thirty-six hours, I get these instant messages: "Hi. How are you?"; "Haven't heard from you in awhile"; "Are you okay?"; *or* "Where are you?" with a big exclamation point! My husband thinks I'm being ridiculous. "Just delete them and don't respond"—that's what he says. I told him, "I tried that, and she just keeps sending me things, and then I feel bad." How do you back off from the Devil? I should just laugh about this, but, honestly, I feel like I'm suffering from PTS—Post Traumatic Stress. Maybe it was all the hats and pencils she stole from me. You're right, you're right. I'm not gonna answer her emails anymore, and that's it. Eventually she'll get the hint and just move on. Okay, let's just turn on the computer and check the sites we need for this project. (*Her emails come up.*) Uh-oh . . . Oh no.

Empty

WOMAN

(*On phone*) Oh my God, honey. Oh, sweetheart, you aren't going to believe it. Don't get upset. Someone broke into our house and took everything. Everything! The policeman thinks it was sometime between . . . Yes, I have the police here now. They're filing a report. Everything is gone. Every valuable we have. Stolen. I just got home twenty minutes ago. The door was locked, so I didn't suspect anything. And . . . I don't know how to tell you this. The dog. The dog is gone. Caesar must have fled when he saw the burglars. He's the worst watch dog ever. I'm sure he'll come home. I know how much you love that dog. Everything is gone—the TV, the computer, the furniture. The furniture! It looks like no one lives here. They're only material things, though. At least we still have each other. The police actually had the gall to ask if we had been fighting lately. Imagine! What does that have to do with it? I don't know where we are going to sleep tonight. We can't sleep here. There's no bed, no sheets, no pillows, no towels, not even dirty towels. Who would want our dirty towels? We can't eat. We have no dishes, no utensils. The wine rack's gone—along with all the wine. They took our food, too. They even took the dog's food. Isn't this supposed to be a good neighborhood? How did they leave with all of that stuff? We don't even know how they got in! There doesn't seem to be any forced entry. You have to see it. Can you come home now? I can't hear you. You sound muffled. Honey, what was that? Does someone have a dog at the office? For a second I thought I heard Caesar. There it is again. What? No, I haven't seen a note. What note?

⸎

My favorite people in the world are actors, with no question. Here's one of many "things" I look for: Is this person nice? Now, by that I don't mean that they have to be Rebecca of Sunnybrook Farm but someone I can share a room with for five to ten weeks. In order for me to do my best work, I need nice.

—Jack Cummings III
Artistic Director, Transport Group

Engaged

YOUNG WOMAN

Chuckie and me are totally hanging out in my dad's den. He was playing PlayStation 3, and I was, like, all morning trying to see if my mother's Tide Stick—you know, the stain remover—could remove my old tattoo from my butt that Chuckie hates because it isn't his name. He's like that. Meanwhile, Marsha is texting me cuz she met this really cute, major hot boy outside the Radio Shack last night, but, like, he ended up to be a jerk because he just thought she would, like, be so ready to get into his car and go down on him—which she did, but how could he know that, right? The conceited moron. So the Tide Stick's kinda working, but I'm starting to itch a little. So I say bye to Marsha cuz—well, cuz—I don't know, and Chuckie yells, "Shit!" and I go, "What?" and I look and he is on his knees on the floor holding this big, I mean major mad big diamond ring in his hand and he says, "Hey, let's get married," and I go, "Get out of here. I mean, are you shitting me? Is this a frickin' marriage proposal?" And he says he found the ring on the floor. My parents had a party Friday night and someone must have dropped it on the rug. It's a shag. So he goes "Yes," and I say, "We're still in high school," and he says, "Then let's be engaged," and I go, "Okay." He puts the ring on my thumb finger cuz this must be made for one of my mother's real fat friends. Then Chuckie starts searching through my parents' rug all happy, like he's digging for gold or something, and I lie down on the rug next to him, cuz it's kinda romantic, but he only found the back to an earring. Oh—and a Canadian nickel. So then my mom busts in without knocking—yeah, please tell me about it—and she wants to know why Chuckie is looking all spazzed and excited on the rug. She has such a suspicious mind. Oh yeah—and my pants are down. Big deal. And I tell her we're getting married, and she starts screaming about how I better not be pregnant. And I tell her, "Don't be mental. I always take precautions." She looks at Chuckie, who just about jumps through the screen and runs down the street like he's on fire. She goes ballistic and tells me Mrs. Baker lost her cubic zirconia Friday night, so I give her Mrs. Stupid Fat-Ass Baker's stupid, fake, fat-rich-lady ring. Then she freaks again cuz my right butt cheek is, like, all bumpy and puffed up and kind of green. When we get to the emergency room, she tells me I'm grounded, and that means I can't leave the house or even make phone calls. So, up hers, the witch. I text Marsha and we figured it out that, no matter what she says, I am still engaged—technically. Right?

Expel Me

YOUNG WOMAN

Ooh, another meeting with the faculty. What did I do to deserve it this time? I am so hoping you expel me and stop threatening to. What do you have to do around here to get expelled? Please just do what you promise. It amazes me that you think it's so weird that I skip school so much. Why should I come here? As far as I see, all the adults are miserable and depressing. All you overeducated grown-ups with all of your degrees and certificates and letters from the president. If you looked so much smarter and happier than Miguel the super, I'd be the first one on the bus in the morning with all of my homework in a smiley-face folder. What does a student have to do to get some action? Plant a bomb in the cafeteria? Come on. Shouldn't you throw me out just for saying that? What is wrong with you people? Throw me out. You, you're the principal. Expel me, please. What are you waiting for? All you seem to do around here is fight with the teachers. I hear you. I hear them. I see the faces they make to each other when you speak. I'm not naming any names. Besides, Mrs. McCarthy has enough problems of her own. Do you guys have, like, meetings where you vote to keep me around so the focus stays off you or something? Get me out of here. Send me to jail. Anything would be better. My parents can't do anything with me, but at least they have the smarts to give up on me. Why can't you? Believe me, you'll be a lot happier. Does your school rating go down if you lose one? It's just one. I'm not taking anybody with me. I don't need to. I don't want to. I have nothing in common with the common. I don't hobnob with the hoi polloi. Brings me down. I'm above it. Above them. Above you. I do like Miguel, the super. We're dating. Psych! That woke you up. We're not really. I've tried. He's happily married, so he spurns my advances. I don't care. I really only wanted to see if all men were perverts if they had the chance to be. He passed, which I can't say about some teachers. Not naming any names—don't sweat it, Baldy—but let's just say I've learned that the more letters you have after your name, the more rights you think you have. To everything. You know what I mean. You know who you are. Is this meeting still in session, or shall I say, "Class dismissed?"

A Family of Means

WOMAN

Suggestion: A Southern touch is nice.

Jim, you don't know. Believe me, I come from a long line of mean people. I mean it. Really mean. They are. You have to know this. It is only fair for you to know. I'm okay, but that's only cuz I'm some kind of mutation or something. Seriously. That's how the story goes, anyways. Mean people from way far back, especially the women. My grandma was so mean they were going to put her in prison, but the judge thought it would be too mean to the prisoners. Well, that's how the story goes about her. She was even scary to look at. I'd show you a picture of her, but they were all destroyed in the house she burnt down. She was mad at my grandpa, so she torched the house with him in it. She said he drank too much, so while he was sleeping she lit a match to his breath. It started an inferno. She said her only regret that day was that she never got her smoke. I've seen the ashes. She kept them with her as a memento. She raised a whole slew of mean kids. She wasn't exactly nice to the kids, either. They were scared stiff all the time. And she didn't even have to yell. She'd just give them the eye when she'd strike a match to light a cigarette. It was to keep them in line, but it made them all bad sleepers. They all grew up to be meaner than Grandma. Yeah, she was the meanest damn grandma in the world. I remember my grandma smiling once. And I was so surprised. She had all these bright, white, perfect teeth. I went right up to her and told her what a beautiful smile she had, and she bit me. Six stitches, right here. She was a witch, and she even looked like one. She knew it, too. She liked it. She told us she flew around over the city at night, looking for victims. When we saw a cat or squirrel run by, she'd say, "That was Mr. So-and-So" or "There goes Miss Whosie-Who. They didn't listen to me." She was the meanest damn grandma in the world. My mom is the nicest one of them all, and you know how scary she is. So, Jim, I want to marry you and have kids, as much as you do, but I don't want you to say that I didn't warn you. 'Cuz I've got some mean genes.

Freckles

MATURE WOMAN

He told me my freckles were age spots. My dermatologist. I was speechless. I've had freckles for years. They were my freckles, not age spots. You can bet your bottom dollar I went to a new dermatologist—a woman this time, thank you. She asked me if I wanted to get rid of my age spots. I went home, poured myself a stiff drink, and said the word aloud: *fifty*. Fifty years old. I say it slowly because . . . because I have to take it in. I mean, only four years ago, I was thirty-five. Alright, I guess it was fifteen years. I guess that's when my freckles became age spots and I lost my memory. What happened? Oh, and get this! I go to the dentist the other day—a new dentist, because my regular dentist *retired*. Anyway, my new dentist says, "How long has that back tooth been like that?" I was like, "All my life." You know what he says? "Wow, it's gotta come out. That's way too old." *Way too old*. He used those words. He must have seen the blood drain from my face. Suddenly he backtracked. "Oh, I meant your tooth, not you." But my tooth is me! My tooth and me are bound together. Just like all my muscles, and bones, and skin, and hair—it's all me, right? And then for a split second I thought maybe it is possible to have an old tooth in a young body. Maybe one tooth *is* fifty years old, but the rest of my mouth is thirty-eight. Gallbladder—fifty. Kidneys—thirty-five. It's like maintaining a car. You know, some parts are old and need replacement, and some parts are brand new. It's crazy, I know, but, for a few seconds, it was comforting. The zenith of my denial about my age was at my twin sister's fiftieth birthday party. Someone said, "I didn't know you were fifty!" And I said, "Oh, we're not identical." Even my husband said the jig was up that night. I have thought about telling people that I'm sixty. Then everyone will think I look fantastic for my age, right? Sixty is the new fifty. Fifty is the new forty. Hey, I just had a thought. If I tell people I'm forty, will they think my age spots are freckles? Oh, it's no use. I do miss my freckles. Fifty. There. I said it again. Five-O . . . with freckles.

⊰⊱

I have frequently watched actors make choices in their auditions that are patently wrong. During the five years I was casting replacements for Vampire Lesbians of Sodom, *I encountered many actors who behaved as if they were refugees from an insane asylum. After sympathetically dismissing them with a polite "Thank you," I might mutter to the stage manager, "Didn't have a clue." But why? Sometimes the issue is talent. More often, however, these actors haven't done their homework. They haven't read the script and therefore have no idea what world they are attempting to inhabit. Careful script analysis should be a part of the preparation for any serious audition. A title can be misleading!*

—KENNETH ELLIOTT, PH.D.
DIRECTOR AND PROFESSOR OF THEATRE

Help Wanted

MATURE WOMAN

Suggestion: She is not deliberately suggestive; she just digs herself deeper into a corner.

Wow, you are in charge of things? You are just better looking than I expected. I think of people working in offices as being all pasty. You look like an outdoorsy, athletic kind of guy. Guess you have weekends off, 'cause you obviously have time to work out. I didn't bring a résumé, sir, mostly because, well, I've never had a job. No, none of any kind. Ever. How old am I? Oh, not very to some and very, very to others—is that a legal question? I just wondered if perhaps I could be disqualified because of my age. Of course, not having any prior experience would be a larger factor. Not that I haven't had experience, of course. I'm a very experienced woman. There's hardly an experience I haven't had, besides this one. Not only have I never had a job, but I've never even interviewed for one. I swear. This is my first time, so please be gentle. Sorry if that sounded like it had any innuendo in any way. I don't want to say anything that might be misconscrewed—strued! I don't mean to sound suggestive. That would be silly, because you might as well be about ten and me a hundred, although an age difference never bothers me—never mind. Could you just give me the job because there is one and I'm here and I want it? Does it work like that? I mean, unless you've promised it to someone else or need to fill a certain quota of some kind based on race or sex or qualifications—something limiting like that. Only kidding. But seriously, could you just give it to me, now, right here? The job, I mean. Of course you know that's what I mean. Could you just use me temporarily? You know, feel me out for a while? I learn by doing. Just give me a go. I'm very hands-on. Try me! You'll be satisfied, I promise. I know there is no job I can't pull off, no matter how big. I mean it. The bigger the better. I mean, not that it has to be big. At all. I don't care if it's small. Maybe it'll grow into something bigger later, you know? Okay, I think I'm done now. I guess that wraps it up. Oh, I'm sorry, have you finished? Good, good. That wasn't too painful. So, how was I?

Hope

WOMAN

Suggestion: This monologue can also be played by a man.

What can I say about Hope? Hope. She . . . Well, growing up, everyone—girls, boys, teachers, parents, clergy—everyone wanted to be around her. Every girl's mother wanted her to be more like Hope. Every boy's mother wanted him to marry Hope. To us, she was a Supreme Being of the Highest Order. Maybe we made too much of her. She certainly didn't ask for it. You know the kind of person who makes everything they do seem glamorous, and then you try it and it goes back to being ordinary? Hope played the clarinet, and every girl wanted to switch to clarinet as soon as Hope took it up. Hope couldn't even play it well, but she made it seem cool. Every dumb thing she touched turned instantly cool, and she never seemed to have to try. She was just at home in herself, always. Hope was magic. Sounds so corny, but just ask anyone who knew her. I emphasize I'm not alone in this. Everyone agrees. Everyone. Hope could have been anything. Everything was so effortless. It came so easy. She had it all in the palm of her hand. The world on a string. She ruled, you know? She was the one—the golden one. You know, the one you could always count on to make sense of everything. When you wanted to poop out, Hope would get you through it. She had a knack for keeping it in perspective. That's why this is . . . I mean, no one would ever . . . I just can't believe . . . You tell me. Just like that. I can't fathom why—why she would just end it. And like that, so swiftly and violently. This is not cool. Excuse me. I . . . I know there is a lesson in this. There must be, but I'm not ready to learn it. Maybe someday I will understand why, but not right now. Inside me, right now, I still need to hold on to the Hope I know.

It's All Good

WOMAN

Thank you. It's alpaca. You know, I heard from my assistant that you were doing this event, and, since I've been practicing Spiritual Serenity for the last six years, I thought, "I've got to do this. I can definitely help raise awareness," you know? So anything I can do to help would be great. Ah, well, I'd rather not talk, but I'd love to present an award or something like that. Anything like that would be great. You know, Spiritual Serenity has changed my life so much that I really want this event to be amazing. So in order to help you help others, I'll just need a few basics, like, um . . . Well, I'll need a car to and from the event. Otherwise, how can I get here? A hair-and-make-up person—I'll provide names to your accountant. And an assistant to my assistant, like an intern or something would be fine. Oh, and three comp tickets to the event, 'cos we want as many people as possible to come, right? So that's it. It's all good. Oh, I forgot. I'll need a private dressing room—not for me but for my stylist. He needs one. He's the one who got me into Spiritual Serenity. He's amazing. You'll love him. So let me ask you, the event starts at seven, right? Because I won't be arriving until sometime after eight, so please make sure that my award presentation doesn't happen until the event is at least half over. Thank you. It's cashmere. Oh, I almost forgot. You know what would really help? When I arrive, it would be so helpful if no one looked directly at me because I just don't want to get too nervous. You understand. And one quick question: Will Spiritual Serenity be taking pictures of the event? Because I do have photo approval. Here's my lawyer's number. You can contact them directly. They're really nice. So this is gonna be fantastic. I can't wait. I'm up for anything you need me to do. Isn't that what's so great about Spiritual Serenity? It inspires generosity of spirit. I'll see you all that night. I'll have my assistant call your office and hammer out details—on paper. It's all good. Thank you. It's lizard.

It's Me, Jessica

YOUNG WOMAN

(*On phone*) Sniper? Sniper? My God, how great it is to hear your voice. It has been way too long. I have been thinking about you nonstop. It was kind of amazing last time. I even wrote a song about it. I'll have it for you when . . . What? Jessica. Jessica Hopkiss. From? From life. We've been together a lot. I see you every time you're in Southern New England. I know you aren't coming here as often lately. But you always sing that song you wrote about me. I hear it on the radio. About the dead bird in flight. Well, actually, I only called just to check up to see how you are doing. Because you looked like hell the last time, no offense. And I expected you to stay the whole night in the motel. So I thought you maybe got sick. And I wanted to make sure you were okay. I guess you are. I'm so happy you are. I am—so happy—you are. There's no reason to be sorry. Because you don't need to be sorry. I know you're a very busy guy and . . . What? You gave me this number. I'm sure you did. It's in my phone book. It's the only number that I have for you. It was written on your rolling papers, and you said I could keep them. Do you have a different number you want me to call? I have no problem with that. You could call me, even, if you are in the surrounding area, you know? I get around. I mean, I could arrange some things and go where you are. Anywhere in the Northeast is easy. New Hampshire is not that far from Boston. Canada, I've done Canada. I saw in the papers that The Hyperdermics played Connecticut a few months ago. I thought, "Wow, The Hyperdermics are playing Hartford. I should try to get to it." But I'm the one sorry that I didn't make it. Forgive me. I was busy. Oh, really? Only the South? No, no. I love the South. Sniper, I can go as south as you want me to go. Sniper? I look forward to it. I can leave school. You kidding? That's easy. I am so flunking anyway. And I can even travel with the band. I don't need a stupid diploma. I'm a songwriter. They never have diplomas. Not the good ones, anyway. Okay, you will? When?

Because I can keep in touch. Do you still have my number? I was thinking maybe you lost it. I can give it to you again. Six one seven, three seven six—okay, you have it. Good. Then I'll wait to hear from you. And I want you to hear the song I wrote, okay? I can even sing it for you—Sniper? Sniper? Oh, don't forget the area code. Six one sev— (*Click*) He has it.

Keep Walking

WOMAN

Suggestion: Works well with rapid-fire, British delivery. This monologue can also be played by a man.

I'll be very clear here. You're all lovely girls, but only one of you gets the contract. So, let's get to work. Carly. Your hair—atrocious. It will come off. Now just walk. Not bad, keep walking, hmmm, pivot, turn—no expression, please. Very good. Ashley. Good bones, good hair—unfortunate height. Walk, keep walking, pivot, turn. Great walk, Ashley. It's just so unfortunate that you're five-foot-six. Can you grow an inch in the next few days? Because that's really what we need from you. Chase. Great name. Good bearing. Unfortunate nose. That will have to be changed if you're even to be considered for a commercial contract. You understand that, don't you? Good. Okay, walk, walk, walk, pivot, turn and finish. Fine. That nose is a problem. Are you Jewish? Is that the problem? Really, you must deal with it, because honestly, Chase, I like you and I think a new nose will exponentially increase your chance for booking. Nurit. You're beautiful, you know it, so let's see you strut your stuff. Walk, walk—okay, you need to learn how to walk. If you don't master this by tomorrow, I'll be asking you to pack before the end of the week. Just letting you know. Where are you from? New Jersey? Well, you may be back there soon. Pivot, turn—there's a lot of work to do there. Linda. Bad name. Just telling you. Great look, however. Love the masculine face. Okay, walk, walk. Your walk says, "Don't look at the clothes. Look at me." We need to see the clothes, so can you make your face go away a bit? Hmmm. The runway is not your friend, but you might be able to get some commercial campaigns for skin care products—for men. Andie. Where are you from again? Kentucky. Oh dear. That accounts for the horsy face. Good bones, right height. Okay, walk, walk, keep walking, pivot, turn. Alright. Very Derby. I'm just going to say it—*Neigh!* (*Makes horse sound*) You've got quite a week ahead of you, Andie. Good Luck. Lissa. Pretty, love the face. Lovely shoulders. Okay, walk, walk, very nice, keep walking. Oh, don't speak, Lissa! Spoils all illusions. Pivot, turn. Very nice, Lissa. If you never speak, you have a good shot. And I do mean never, Lissa. Paula. Again, unfortunate name. Can you change it? Let's call you Paloma from now on. Have your parents change it as soon as possible. Okay, walk, walk. Lovely, lovely. Great walk, Paloma. Now let me say this. Your face is rather distorted, but with the name Paloma it becomes a bit Cubist, and that can be your signature. You've got something there, Paloma. Capitalize. Billie. I like you, Billie, and I love the whole lesbian slant to the name. Okay, walk, walk. See the confidence, girls? It says, "I'm not at all pretty and I know it, but I can turn the whole thing around and make the runway about my nonlooks." Pivot, turn. Well, you may frighten some bookers, but with the right campaign you might become a star. Maria. Ah, Maria, Maria. Can you be a bit more Anglo? Frankly I think being Latin is just so over. Also, your boobs are getting in your way. Your curves are a terrible distraction, Maria. I suggest getting rid of them right away. Don't work out or eat this week. So, girls, as you can see, you all have your work cut out for you. Tomorrow, eight A.M. sharp, you need to be here for evaluation of commercial viability from our panel of experts. Keep your chins and spirits up, and welcome to the world of modeling. I know this has been tough, girls, but I tell you all this because, honestly, I care. I care deeply.

Whether your audition is the result of an open call or an agency submission, from the moment you walk through that door, the time is yours. Make the most of it by taking full possession of your monologue or song. By that, I mean try to find the joy in the telling of your story, be it through text or song. Too many actors fall into the trap of focusing on the casting director or other decision-makers, concerning themselves unnecessarily with how they are being perceived and what type of response they may or may not be getting. This will only serve to rob you of your joy. After all, we are performers because we love to perform. My advice is: Don't wait for an acting job to give you the opportunity to shine. Let your love of storytelling fuel your audition. In this way, the folks behind the table become passengers on your journey, even if it's only a sixteen-bar journey! In the end, they may choose you or another actor. You have no control over those decisions. But, they will *remember you.*

—ANDREA FRIERSON
ACTOR/WRITER

The Korean Lesbian

YOUNG ASIAN WOMAN

I am a complete stereotype for a Korean. Guess what my father did? You're right! He owned a Korean deli, and we lived above it. I've probably skinned ten thousand carrots for that salad bar. We came over here when I was about three, so I learned everything about the world from that place. How to count money, what Americans liked, and, of course, how to speak English. So now I speak better English than most of my dad's customers, and I'm great in math. Big surprise, right? I told ya—a stereotype. Fourteen hundred combined on the SATs. It's all silly, I guess. (*Pause*) Yes, I love the park at this time of the year, too. The buds are just about to burst. Just about to burst. See, I can't make my parents understand. I have no desire whatsoever to go to college right now. Of course, my parents want me to go to Harvard or Yale, and I probably could go to either one of those schools, but . . . But I'm in love with a twenty-seven-year-old woman from Ireland that I met at the Gay and Lesbian Center. She's a sculptor. She shows her work all over the world. I want to go off to Ireland and be with her, and she wants that, too, but I know that this will just kill my parents, who—oh, by the way, did I mention that my parents don't even know that I'm gay yet? I keep meaning to tell them, but for so long I didn't do anything with my gayness, so I thought, "Why should I tell them anything when nothing is happening?" I'm thinking of telling them that I got a scholarship to study abroad and then slowly introducing them to the idea of my lifestyle once I'm over there. My cousin, who knows my whole deal, thinks I'm nuts. He thinks I should forget about Kate—that's my girlfriend's name—and go to Harvard, which is totally lesbian anyway, and just tell my parents that I'm gay after I've won some big award or something—you know, to balance out their disappointment. Trust me, they will be disappointed. They don't like anything that cracks a mold. What my cousin doesn't understand is the depth of my feelings for Kate. Look, I know I shouldn't talk about depth when I'm just eighteen, but, honestly, I am just overwhelmed by this woman. She just makes me feel like I don't . . . like *anything* in the world is possible. I know that everything in the world points to this being just a mad crush, not logical, certainly not forever and all that. I get it, I get it. But isn't there something to be said for doing something that is just so totally illogical, so spontaneous, so rushed and romantic and fun and crazy and, God, isn't eighteen the time to do that? I mean, Harvard will always be there, but a cottage outside Dublin with a gorgeous, red-haired artist might not be. Do you see my point? I guess you never thought you'd be spending your lunch hour listening to some raving lesbian stranger with love issues. I'm sorry. I will. I will. Maybe I will.

Last Call

WOMAN
Suggestion: This monologue can also be played by a man.

Oh, thank God. I was afraid you were going to tell me you weren't drinking anymore, either. No one seems to drink anymore. Everywhere you go, everyone thinks they're an alcoholic. What is that, a new term for "party pooper"? Can make you feel self-conscious, you know? I don't like feeling self-conscious. I'm not ashamed. I don't apologize to anyone. I'll tell you that right now. I will say flat out, I love a glass of sherry, maybe more than I love anything. More than anything. Or anyone. That sounds weirder than it is. It's just that, at the end of the day, a glass of sherry is just nice to come home to. It's reliable. For that matter, I love a cold beer or two on a hot afternoon. So what? And a dry martini with extra olives before the theatre. They don't let you drink during. (*Laughs*) I love wine with dinner. Everything tastes better with wine. I'm not much of a cook; sometimes I skip the dinner. I like an occasional aperitif. After all, it aids digestion—and boring conversation. Then maybe have a cup of coffee—preferably Irish. The best contribution the Irish made is their coffee. Enough said. But seriously, I'd rather stay in bed than go to a brunch without a Bloody Mary waiting for me. So there. I won't go on about it, but it has tomato juice, which is good for you. It's got vitamin C. That's all, except beer comes from grains, doesn't it? It's all weedy and malty. It's downright health food, for Chrissake. What can I say? It has hops. So what's all this crap about? Why is getting a nice buzz getting such a bad rap? It's not like you have to get in a car and drive someone home. I never do. I'm pretty much the designated drinker. Cut me a break, because you ain't getting me to go to no Party Poopers Unanimous. I'm not slamming anybody. It isn't like I'm totally, teetotally intolerant. Oh, no. I say, live your life straight up or on the rocks. And if your glass is half empty, fill it up, for Chrissake. Enjoy it. Enjoy it. Life should be a party. Here's a toast to the last of us, the ones who hold on tight to their ancestry. We are proud of our bloodlines—no matter what the legal percent alcohol level. So bottoms up until we bottom out! Cheers!

Late for Rehearsal

WOMAN

I'm here! I'm here! Sorry I'm late for the rehearsal. I had to stop for gas—self-serve. Too bad you couldn't start without me. You did? But I'm the bride. It's "Here Comes the Bride," remember? Anyway, I'm here. Honey, I'm here. Do I look okay? Yes? Just okay? I just thought you might say "beautiful." But that's okay. I'm ready to go with the rehearsal. Let's start. But maybe you should marry someone you think is beautiful. I'm kidding. I'm kidding. Because, after all, I'm just okay. I'm sorry. Honey, I'm just so stressed. It's raining. I'm getting a cold sore. Did I tell you I had to pump my own gas? I'm sorry, honey. I love you so much, baby. I said, "I love you so much, baby." Baby, why didn't you say "I love you so much" back? Well now you're just saying it because you were instructed. Not that it doesn't count—just not quite as much. I know it's late. What do you mean I'm holding everybody up? Isn't there enough time for a little acknowledgment of love the night before our wedding? Are you sure you want this wedding? One hundred percent sure you want to commit? "Yes"? That's what you say to me? "Yes"?! Well, that just doesn't cut it. When I say something sweet and loving, you should top it. Not repeat it. *Top it.* I repulse you, don't I? You loathe me! You are trying to get out of this! "No"? That's your answer? No, you don't want to get out of it? That's not very reassuring. You need to be more demonstrative, more passionate about it. You should need to show me how much you need me, want me. Prove it to me now. Why don't you take me in your arms, forget all propriety and reason, throw me down right now and take me, take me on that empty pew, right here in front of the altar . . . Oh, hello, Father. Sorry I was running a little late. I am so sorry I've been holding everybody up and all. I'm so nervous and jittery. All at once I'm breaking down, breaking out, and breaking up. And did I mention I'm premenstrual? 'Cause I didn't mean to. I'm sorry. How do I look? Beautiful? *Thank you!* How beautiful?

The Latest Chapter

MATURE WOMAN

Doctor, my daughter is a very good actress. It's the one thing I'll take credit for. She has unfortunately taken all the advantages that she was given—and believe me, there were many—and thrown them back into everyone's faces. I appreciate your concern for my daughter's health and well-being, but, believe me, this latest "suicide attempt," as you call it, was yet another one of her attention-seeking ploys. She's taken pills before, you see, so obviously she is not really serious. We all know that if someone is dead-set about being dead, they can jump off a roof or shoot themselves in the mouth. They don't take pills. Margaret has been a problem from the day she was born, I'm afraid. This is just the latest chapter. She was a colicky baby, an uncontrollable adolescent, and now a troubled and delinquent teenager. I cannot have her disrupting the family like this, so what do you suggest? Therapy!? My dear doctor, Margaret has seen some of the best therapists in the country, two of them here and two of them in New York. They've given up on her. No, no, no, the talking cure cures no one. I believe in tough love. It's how I grew up, and look where it got me. Well, doctor, I suppose I should be very grateful that you saved my daughter's life, but I will tell you right now I plan on collecting her and her things tonight and packing her off to a very strict boarding school. Fresh air and discipline—that's what Margaret needs, not coddling and indulgence. Thank you for all your medical support for now, but I will be taking over my daughter's care from here on in. Good day.

The Layout

MATURE WOMAN

I will say it again: no, no, and no! How could you have approved this layout? This layout is so uninspired, it is beyond prosaic. It did not move me on any level except maybe to vomit. We are supposed to be not only the last word in fashion but also the first, second, and third. The September layout is not just another layout. It has to be the Eiffel Tower, the Statue of Liberty, and Bilbao all in one issue. *Everything* that happens in the culture that we are living in right now is filtered through this magazine. I can only assume you were high on some sort of psychotropic drug when you approved of this because there is no other reason for it. Get out of my office and don't enter it again until you can astonish me! I am not going to upset myself further about this. I am going to remain calm. I will meditate, relax, and go deep deep deep within myself. But not too deep. (*She closes her eyes and starts to chant.*) Ohmmmmmm . . . (*Her eyes manically pop open.*) *Fire everyone that was involved with that layout!* Whoever is outside my office right now, come in here immediately! Who are you? Well stop cleaning and take notes! This layout has to be spectacular. I just had a vision while meditating—something fresh but not self-conscious. I want dreamy images with an edge. It has to be utterly modern but hearken back to the past—but no nostalgia! I hate nostalgia. Oh, I have a headache, a terrible terrible headache! Oh, you have some pain pills? How utterly wonderful. (*She takes some pills.*) Thank you, thank you, what is your name? Rosa Rosa Rosa, thank you. I can tell just by looking at you that you understand the depth of my despair over this layout. Pain, that's right, Rose . . . Rosa. Utter utter pain. No one really understands what it is like to run the world's most formidable fashion-authority magazine. It is not just a job, not just a career—it is a calling. A vocation. All that is beautiful and good is represented in this magazine. And with the September issue, we will tell the world what is beautiful and good. Do you have any more of those pills? For later, of course. Thank you, Rose . . . Rosa.

When people buy this magazine, they are telling the world, "I have made a choice—a choice to live in the world of inspiration and grandeur." People who read our magazine are not interested in just the mere or the small. They are interested in elevating themselves, not only because the blouses in our magazine are two thousand dollars but because they are reaching for something higher, something that will allow them to leave this world just a little better than how they came into it. I can tell just by looking at you, Rosa, that you understand every word that I am saying. Meditate with me, Rosa, so that we can send out all these inspiring vibrations to the rest of the world. (*She closes her eyes and places a hand over her heart.*) Ohmmmmmm . . . We have to get a refill for those pain pills first thing, and then we have to introduce you as my new second-in-command. I adore you, Rosa, and you must be at my side at every moment. Oh, this is going to be wonderful. I have finally found someone who can truly assist me without disruptions and disagreements. You are a listener. A true listener. That's what I have needed all this time. Someone who doesn't speak but listens and listens and listens and listens.

I love auditioning! Each time it's a chance to act, to meet people, to get cast, or to plant seeds for other jobs. It's a privilege, really, to have the opportunity. My singing teacher, Ed Dixon, who works on Broadway all the time, told me that, every single day, he sings his audition songs full-out. What that told me is that the more prepared you can be, the less nerves take over. It's totally true! Being as prepared as I can possibly be makes the whole process less nerve-racking and more fun.

—Susan Varon
Actor/Writer/Acting Coach

The Lead

YOUNG WOMAN

It's a problem. That's why I'm asking your advice. I mean, look at me! I'm never gonna get those juicy character roles. Those are the roles I want, but they seem beyond me. I'm always cast as the lead! It's so discouraging. My therapist told me that my beauty is actually holding up my development as an artist, and I believe her. If you're too good-looking, they won't let you grow. Okay, sure, I get the leads and usually the most money, but that's not gonna necessarily get me any awards. You saw Kate Winslet on *Extras*. You have to play a blind person or a retard to get awards, and I'm just not getting those parts. I want to be taken seriously. Nobody takes very attractive people seriously. My agent told me that I lost out the last two roles because, one, I was too young and, two, I was too beautiful. That hurt. It really is a terrible burden. So you're lucky, Suzanne. You're old enough to be someone's mother but young enough to still be sexually active. You're not beautiful, but you definitely could be with, like, a range of guys—the nerd, the sweet guy, the thug. Me? Always with the leading man. It's boring. And your figure is perfect for TV. You're fat, but you're TV-fat, which means in real life you're just a tad overweight. You can be the friend, the sister, the neighbor, the relative, the coworker, the boss. You can get so many more parts. I'm limited to the star romantic lead who gets the guy in the end after we go through a rough patch. Is that interesting? I don't think . . . Hey, Suzanne, where are you going? I thought you were my friend. I need you. I rely on you for advice. I'm in crisis, and you're walking away? Here I am in pain about my career, and you're leaving? Well, the next time you have a problem, Suzanne, don't bother to call me because I'll be too busy—too busy playing the lead on some hot new TV show or romancing my new leading man while you're . . . you're auditioning for some guest spot on a show for the USA Network. I don't need friends who can't be sympathetic to my problems. And let me tell you something else, Suzanne. The world doesn't revolve around secondary players. It revolves around leads—like *me!*

A Little Late

MATURE WOMAN

You married me, Joe, and you shouldn't have. You went and you took me down the aisle on my father's arm. You didn't love me the way you said. The way you promised. You couldn't have ever meant it, even at the time. What am I to think, I'm asking you? It isn't like you didn't know about yourself and your personal leanings. You even showed some behaviors to the like. But Joe, my God, I was twenty-two and wanting to have a family, and you said it so joyfully—that God brought me to you. You were so convincing. And then what did you expect? That you would be made into another flesh when we swore to each other that day in front of God and family? Did you think a miracle was going to happen then? When? During the consecration? What could you have thought? I was hopeful and happy. Everyone was happy—except for my dad. It was a hot day in June, but he was shaking like he saw the devil. Maybe he did. Maybe he suspected something and didn't have the heart to tell me. But you knew. You knew all along. You didn't have a dyspeptic stomach all those years. You didn't want to get close. When I think of all the barley water I had you drink. You just didn't want to be like that with me. There was always an excuse. You should have abandoned me right then, Joe, or at least when you started carrying on, in that way, all those years ago with those *sorts* you are telling me about. Telling me now just makes you look conniving and me look silly and sad. I feel I've been had. Only not the way I would have liked. I wanted you to have me in that way women speak about. I always hoped you would. Maybe if you did, with me, just let yourself enjoy it, you would have grown to like it more. There were other men who wanted me like that, you know. Two very good ones, too. But I only wanted to be with you—no one else. We shared the same values, didn't we? Don't we? I have always loved you, Joe. I still can't imagine myself with anyone else. You are so good to me, so sweet, and you needed me so much always. Now I know why. Why couldn't you stay in the closet with the rest of the dirty laundry? Why now? Why not just continue? No one has to know. Why this sudden need to be truthful, Joe? What is good about it? Nothing. I can't just stop loving you, just like that. I'm not about to leave you—not at this time in my life. You aren't—are you . . . are you . . . leaving me—you aren't—for this person? This guy? Is this why? Because it doesn't have to change anything for him or you. We will get through this. What you do behind my back is none of my business. I won't ask any questions. There are worse problems to have. If it weren't this, then it would be something else, wouldn't it? Everybody has something to overcome. Even with this to work through, we're still in better shape than most people.

Maturity

YOUNG WOMAN

David, I'm sorry. I don't want it to be like this. I'm so . . . Oh, God. This is exactly what I didn't want to happen. Don't confuse me. Let me just say this. I can't be something I'm not. I'm twenty-three years old. I can't even be twenty-four until I actually am. Well, if you want maturity, then date someone your own age. I can't be some woman who has all this knowledge and wisdom and "old soul-ness" that you are so in love with *and* be twenty-three! I'm sorry, but it doesn't work that way. I know I need to get things going, but right now living where I live and working at this store is where I'm at. I got through graduate school, didn't I? Yes, with your help, but I also worked really hard. I have learned a lot from you, David. I have, and living together might just be amazing, but come on—let's be real here. You barely tolerate most of my friends as it is. Can you imagine if they were around our apartment? David, why are you making this so difficult? I love you, too, but sometimes there are just too many obstacles. I know I'm messed up, but the one thing I'm clear about is that I am messed up, and guess what? A lot of twenty-three-year-olds need a lot of room to figure out what we are doing, and moving in with my forty-year-old former professor is not going to help me! I'm sorry. Oh, God. Please just don't call me for a while. Maybe we can be . . . Maybe after some distance we can . . . Please, David, let me go.

No Flowers

MATURE WOMAN

Here I am. I almost didn't make it, but, at last, here it is: Restful Overlook Cemetery, Lot 207, Section C, Plot 722X. What the hell is that? Couldn't they have pretty names for where we bury people? I never would have even found it if it weren't for that nice man over there with the shovel. (*Waves to man in distance*) So here I am, standing in the middle of a cemetery staring at your grave, and I still don't believe it. Here you are, supposedly right here, in this spot. That's what I'm told. Why don't I feel anything? There's your name. There it is, carved right there. And there's my name, too, right next to it, which is weird to see. But thank you, I guess. That was very considerate of you, and I'm glad we'll be buried together, and it saves everyone a lot of trouble, but did you have to put my date of birth? Damn it. You know how I am about my age. I always lie about it. I've been lying about it for so many years, I'm surprised you even remembered it. While you were at it, why not put my height, weight, and Social Security number? Oh, so what. It isn't important. No one will believe it anyway. I look so good. And it isn't like it's etched in stone or anything—ha-ha. What am I doing? No one could ever tell me that I would come here, alone, and talk out loud like this. How strange. I mean, this isn't like me at all, and I can't stop. I feel like I'm trapped in a cliché, talking to my deceased husband like this. It is so not me. Why do I keep talking out loud? Can you just hear my thoughts? I hope not, because sometimes what I think is pretty disturbing. I never even knew I was capable of such thoughts. But this isn't you buried here really. It can't be. I feel no presence of anything. Oh, where are you? Where? This is not supposed to be. Well, at least I didn't come with flowers, a bunch of stupid daisies or something. That would be just so movie-of-the-week. And, of course, you didn't believe in cutting flowers. You thought it was mean. What kind of a man thinks that? Please don't answer. That would really freak me out. Seventeen years is a long time to be with anyone. I really liked it. I appreciate all the plants you gave me. They're nice. They're doing well, too. I love them. Every one. Especially the azalea. Maybe I should plant one right here. Right in front of my age. What do you think? I just wish I could feel you. Could you give me a sign? Something? Right now? Lightning would be good. Could we get some of that? Some angry sky to open up. Torrents of raging waters crashing down. That would be a nice touch. Oh my God, is it really starting to rain? It is. I feel a drizzle—just a drizzle, like a mist. Maybe that's you. A mist. Of course, of course. You're mist. You are missed, more than you'll ever know. Ahhhh. Look at me trying to be poetic and adorable here. It's hard to be adorable alone. My hair is getting frizzy, thanks to you. But this mist feels—okay.

The Pretty Girl

WOMAN
Suggestion: Exude genuine Southern charm with this one.

Charlie, you always had a notion. Honey, I remember you sassing my mama about my communion dress, saying it wasn't pretty enough and that it needed more lace. Didn't you even demand that Mama put some sparkles on it or something? Appliqués! That's it—lace appliqués. Nobody's been a better friend to me, Charlie, and these past four months—well, they've just been hot-dog fabulous! Wait till I tell the gang back in Shreveport that I was in the ladies room with Calista Flockhart and that she didn't look so good! I'm so sorry, Charlie, 'cos it's been so much fun being with you and all, but I just gotta go home. Now hear me out. See, you always knew you wanted to leave Louisiana, and look at you now—Hollywood Stylist to the Stars! I'm so proud of you, Charlie. We all are. And honestly, if something had landed in my lap, why hell, I'd take it! But you know, Charlie, what I've noticed out here is people work awful hard for something . . . well, something not too solid. You're lucky, Charlie. You always knew what you wanted and grabbed it. But me? Well, I was just happy being your friend who you thought was so pretty. Charlie, I'm not a model or an actress. I'm just a former Shreveport State Fair Junior Miss. I know it doesn't seem very glamorous, Charlie, but I wanna go back home. I miss everything about it: the people, the food, the magnolias, the pelicans. Hell, I even miss the bugs. I just breathe better is all, even with the sulfur smell. I guess I'm just a small-town girl at heart, Charlie. It doesn't mean I can't still wear Prada shoes. I just don't have to wear them all the time.

Be polite, be funny, be courteous, ask questions, and knock 'em dead—even if you feel that those behind the desk are not necessarily giving you the same in return. If you have what the director is looking for, s/he will see it and take note.

—Carl Andress
Director/Author

Sparkle

WOMAN

Suggestion: This monologue can also be played by a man.

Tonight is the night, Juju. I am so excited. Don't be nervous, baby. There is no reason to be. Okay? It's just stage fright. It'll pass. Your costume looks just adorable. Of course you look round. You're a snowflake. The most beautiful snowflake in the entire third grade, however. The rest of the snowflakes pale in comparison. They pale. They're just flakes. Every one. Just remember to smile. Big smile. Remember you are on camera the whole time. Daddy's in the front row with the digital. Don't look directly into it. Smile—big smile. Stop touching your hair. It's perfect. That's because of the spray. It is supposed to feel like cardboard. That's the point. Don't be nervous. You'll perspire. Look at me. It runs in the family. We sweat, so knock it off. Stay calm. Let the audience melt, not you. Think pretty thoughts. Pretty, pretty thoughts. And don't forget to look out at the audience so we can capture your presence, which is all you need. Don't make that face. It'll freeze like that. Not cute, even on a snowflake. When you enter, we are going to applaud, so hold for it, like I told you. Never worry about holding anyone up. You're in the front. They get their cue from you. You can do anything you like. But don't look at your feet. Looks bad, not confident. Whatever you do, remember you are the star snowflake. Because I said so. You stand out. Remember, no two snowflakes are alike. Did you know that? Let me fill you in. On all the snow-covered peaks in all the world, not two, not two are alike. I know all the snowflakes are supposed to be the same in this show. Don't you think I know that? Why do you think you're wearing sequined tights? Don't touch. They're not supposed to be comfortable. Now let's get going, or the bus we arranged to pick up all those people is going to get there before us. And you have to remember that all of these people have come to see you. And you have to remember all of the people have traveled very far just to see you. Only you. So smile, sparkle, and shine at all times. Starting now. Thatta girl. And relax.

Split

WOMAN

I'm not going to raise my voice. I'm going to say it nicely. Jason, get the cat, and let's go. We're leaving, and the cat lives at your house, not mine. You're lucky I let you bring that animal into my home. Your mother seems to think you need to have it with you for comfort, so it is a concession I make when you stay here with me and your dad. But time is up. Step on it, Jason. Put her in the carrying case, which I am not touching—never have and never will—and let's get going. Your mother wants you back by six, and we're expecting dinner guests. Do you hear me? You're not going to make me scream. Let your mother scream, not me. I have learned that there is more power in the whisper. And I'm going to get results. You know why? Because if you don't do as I say, I'm going to kill your cat. Yes I will. I'll bury her in the backyard behind the shed with all the other dead pets. She'll just be another little casualty of a messy divorce. Here, kitty, kitty. Very good, Jason. I knew you'd see it my way. Now wasn't that easy? Wait. Don't forget that horrendous scratch-post thing. Thank you. Now get your ass in the car, or I'll tell your dad how you play with Barbies. Good boy. See how you can catch more flies with honey? It's a valuable lesson.

Waiting

MATURE WOMAN

Suggestion: This monologue can also be played by a man.

He's going to graduate school. You have to graduate from something first before you do that. You graduate, then you go graduate again. Sounds crazy, but some people go in for that sort of thing. I hope I don't smell or anything. (*Sniffs clothes*) I don't want to smell like a loser, you know? He sounds so like—I don't know—like he's gotten a lot of education. Going on to graduate school. Hey, that's pretty good. I haven't seen him—God—since he was three or four. I can't remember, really. But he wants to see me. It's okay. I just don't know what to say to him. I hope he doesn't remember. I don't remember. I'm keeping myself clean today. Nope, I'm not having a drop. I don't know why he found me. He says he doesn't want anything from me. That wouldn't be right, coming to find me so I can give him something, like I owe him something. I haven't seen him since he was—maybe four. I remember he was pretty smart. He talked a lot, like as soon as he was born. He was one of those talking babies. He used to ask a lot of questions. "What's that? What's that?" That I remember, because it was "What's that?" over and over like a broken record. I don't remember much else about him. I could give him twenty dollars. But I'll see. He said he just wants to meet me once. I guess once'll do him. I can do that. I haven't smoked in two days, because there is nothing very nice about a person who smells of yesterday's tobacco. I smoked one today, but that's fresh. It's different. It isn't really a loser smell if it's today's tobacco on you. It's when it's in your clothes for a season or so . . . He still has seven minutes. He'll show up. I almost didn't, but he's different from me, I guess. He was with those people since he was seven. They adopted him. That's good. I hope he doesn't remember anything else. I wasn't so—you know—I guess he was three or four. I don't remember. Okay. Maybe I'll have some gum. Or no. Well, maybe I'll wait and ask if he wants a piece first. If he does, I will. If he doesn't chew gum, then I won't. 'Cause both people should either be chewing or not chewing, I think. Otherwise, it's just sort of awkward, especially if no one is talking. Okay. Graduate school is very good. I'm just going to give him the twenty. He could probably use the twenty. (*To self*) Okay. Okay. Okay.

White Gloves

MATURE WOMAN

Is it just me, or has the world become just plain uncivilized? Carol, I went shopping today, and, honestly, I came home depressed. Everything I looked at was ugly and poorly made, the service was nonexistent, and the crowds were just horrible. I'm exhausted, and I didn't even get anything. Oh, and remember that little café they had on the fifth floor? They served tea and biscuits. It's a thong boutique now. Carol, I guess I'm just too old-fashioned. I want white gloves to come back. I miss them. Remember how they always finished a look? It doesn't matter what you wear, you put on white gloves and you are good to go. Why did they ever go out of style? For one thing, they're hygienic. You can shake hands, pick up things from the floor, play with other people's pets—do all those things with confidence. You don't have to dash immediately into some restroom to wash your hands. I mean, we keep hearing about all the viruses and germs that are out there—West Nile, Asian Flu, to say nothing of the common cold. And that antibacterial stuff is just too vile, like acrylic medicine for your hands. White gloves are so perfect. Jackie Kennedy always wore white gloves, and she's still a style icon. You loved her, too? You see? They're economical, too. It saves a ton on manicures, right? Who has time for manicures? But you know, Carol, the real reason I miss white gloves? They made people nicer. When you wear white gloves, you become a better person. Think about it, Carol. When I wore white gloves, I never cursed, I stood straighter, and I even had a better vocabulary. Let's start a white gloves club. Who knows? Maybe it'll take. The White Glove Brigade—bringing civil society back one glove at a time! But I have to admit, Carol, I did pick up a couple of thongs as well.

⁂

The central purpose of all auditions is for the actor to succeed.

As a director, I expect the actor to make my casting decision seem insightful and inevitable. In the process, however, the actor is in the vulnerable position of revealing his deeply personal instinct to the artistic judgment of a stranger. Auditions are a bold exercise in trust. And the only way to win the role.

If an actor squanders his audition on fear, he deprives us of our first opportunity for collaboration.

As an actor, I have to remember my own advice when I walk up to the other side of the table.

—WALTER BOBBIE
DIRECTOR/ACTOR

The Bad Deal

MAN

Jack, we can't do this. It's a bad deal, I'm telling you. This company is not worth it, and we're gonna end up saddled with a ton of debt. The whole thing stinks. Who cares what the old man thinks? He's dying, for Christ's sake. Jack, his mind is going and going fast. This is an unsound business decision, and you know it. Dad raised us to make good judgments. This is a bad deal. Look, I know you feel sorry for the guy, but that's not how to run a business—a business that Dad worked his whole life to build up and, I might just say, is the future for both our families. Why is this such a thing for you, Jack? Just because he asked you to do it? If Dad said, "Hey, guys, I want you to take all that money we made and give it to that whore over there so I can have a last thrill," would you do it? Of course not. You would stop him, right? I'm telling you this merger would be like throwing money at a whore. What are you saying, Jack? That I'm not being a good son? That's what I'm trying to be. How can you say this? I'm . . . I'm flabbergasted. Look at me. Jack, look at me! It's not about money. I'm your brother, for Christ's sake. He loved us equally. What the hell are you saying? I don't believe this. Oh no, you're not gonna walk away from me. Jack, we are going to settle this. Please . . . for Dad . . . for us! I don't believe this, I don't believe this.

Before the Fall

MAN

Hey, man. Good morning. Anything you can spare? Have a nice day. God bless you, sir. Thank you, anyway, sir. That's okay. I'm not mad. Anger is a sin. A deadly sin that I don't have in my collection. Hello. Any change today? Thanks, man, for the change. Thank you kindly. Any dollars? Checks? Just asking. Change is good. Have a good day. We all have our limits. I harbor no wrath. Hey, sister, you're lookin' fine. Mmmm-hmmm. Got anything for me? You don't have to give anything. You give me plenty to think about. Proud Mary, keep on walkin'. I got all I need from you. Lust is a deadly sin I don't mind having in my collection. I got no pride for sure. Lust, yeah. Pride, no. Pride comes before the fall. And the fall comes before the winter, when I need a jacket. Gets cold. Gotta get busy. Sir, anything? I'll take anything, as long as it's in cash, check, money order, American Express, or any other legal tender. Or illegal. I'm not choosy. Well, you've got a kind face, ma'am. Very kind indeed. You'd never know by looking how cheap you are. Keep walking. That's right. You want to save time along with your money. Don't worry. God loves cheapskates, or he wouldn't have made so many of you. Just saying the truth. Don't worry. Doesn't cost you nothing to hear it. I give it out for free. What you looking all like that, dude? I don't bite. We're all brothers, man. We're all one world here. We are all in the same boat, with Noah and the animals—and the vegetables. Losers and winners. Saints and sinners. Together. We cannot be proud. I'm not proud. No pride. Pride comes before the fall. Just like summer. Then, after the fall comes winter. I need a jacket. Don't you want to clothe the naked? We all get the goose bumps all over when we're cold. We all feel the heat when there's cops, don't we? Clothe the naked—going once, going twice. Look at you, mama. You are fine. Don't nobody clothe you, I hope, when you're naked. That would be a sin I'd want to stick around for. I could love you. Love you up good. We gotta love each other. One by one or two by two.

Whatever is your pleasure. Like Noah on that Love Boat, man. Proud Mary, I want to go rolling on the river alone with you. Fuck Noah, man. He had two foxes on that raft already. You are fine and mine, baby. No disrespect. You ain't a cop, are you? Cuz I need a cop. Please, somebody, help. I was just beat up. I was jumped by three white ladies in pantsuits. They took everything. See them run? She hit me in the head with a soccer ball, man. No shit. I ain't lying. Lying's a sin. Seventh Commandment. No lying, said God. Thou shalt not lie or steal. I don't steal. I beg and borrow, but they ain't sins—just annoying as hell. I'm going to stop borrowing soon. It stinks. You gotta give back all that shit. We're all together. We all live in a yellow submarine. We are all just sons of Noah and the storm's coming and I need a raincoat. And the Lord said, "Let there be light." Buddy, you got a light? Oh, great. Thank you. Have any smoke, man? No smoke? Then what am I gonna do with the fuckin' matches with nothing to smoke? No, forget it then. I just thought if you had one you'd have the other. You know, where there's smoke, there's fire. Can ya get me some smoke? Then keep going. Get out of here or I'll beat your ass. You're not a cop are you?

The Bike

MAN

I'm not taking the call. I don't want anything to do with him. It's my wish not to speak to him, okay? Honor my wish and just hang up. Or better yet, let him hang on. Let him hang on hold, in Limbo somewhere. You seem to think I have some unfinished business with my father. I don't. You think I need closure. I'm way past that. Closure is just a fancy word for not giving a shit about something you once gave a shit about. I don't need anything from him. It's not like I need him to donate his blood or anything. I've got enough of that crap running through my veins. That's all he ever gave me. I'm not bitter, and that was a long time ago. I don't even know him. Last time I talked to him, it was my ninth birthday. He told me he was coming to see me. He told me he had a bicycle for me, a Schwinn silver three-speed. The people I was living with at the time said I could keep it on the porch. They even bought me a lock so it wouldn't get stolen and a basket for the back and streamers for the handlebars. He kept asking what time I got out of school and for me to meet him by the monkey bars. I don't know why we thought he was telling the truth. He hardly ever came to visit, and never at the scheduled time. And never, ever sober. But that ninth birthday, I believed him. I was in the fourth grade. I watched the clock tick away all day long. This time it was different, and he told me he bought it. A Schwinn. Silver, three-speed. He kept asking what time I got out of school. I couldn't wait. He'd teach me how to ride. Right in the schoolyard, in front of all the other kids. Three speeds. Hand gear. A bicycle, a dad, a cake with candles. We waited till dusk. My father never came. He never called. Not even once, not even drunk. I finally walked home with my foster brother and we put on our birthday hats. There was birthday cake, birthday candles, and, best of all, a birthday wish. I don't know if I was in league with God or the Devil, but I knew my wish would come true. I knew then, as I know now, I will never have to hear his drunken promises ever again. So when or if he calls back, tell him the party's over and he missed it.

The Booking

YOUNG MAN

Why we'd do it? What do you think? We needed the dough. You understand, me and my sister live with a no-good drunk who flat-out told us he doesn't want us around. We take up too much of his cereal. And my sister, y'know, I gotta be there for her. She's a little slow and—well, you've seen my sister. She's ugly. She ain't never gonna get some guy to take care of her and all. I'm all she's got. That's why I thought this was a good idea. I swear I don't see the crime in it. Nobody gets hurt. Everyone benefits. In fact I'd go so far as to say I was providing this neighborhood with a very decent service. The Butt-Ugly Club—that was the name. It was a club for ugly people. We were even mentioned on Howard Stern. That was a big moment for me. Howard's the Man! My sister, she was crying she was so happy that we were getting that kind of attention. I think you got us all wrong. We were providing a valuable service. Do you know how many stupid, ugly people are out there? A lot. A lot. And they ain't never gonna have wives and husbands and girlfriends and all. Some of those people ain't never gonna have sex. See, that's where we came in. We could give them that. These ugly guys felt comfortable with my sister. She's ugly, they're ugly. Nobody's—uh, what's the word—intimated. Yeah, intimidated. Whatever. Everyone's comfortable. It ain't pimping. It's an opportunity. And I'll tell ya something else: there are people out there, they love an ugly girl, they specifically want an ugly girl. My sister was never happier in her life. Who are you to say what she was feeling? She was having sex, getting gifts and money. She was smiling a lot. And you wanna take this away from her. Let me tell ya something: sixteen ain't minor in our neighborhood. You guys don't know nothing. You're just sitting here in these offices. You don't know shi—Why don't you arrest my father? That's your criminal. Made our lives a living hell, drove my mother to an early grave, drinks away all his disability but you arrest me? I'm an entrepreneur, for Christ's sake! But go ahead, arrest me! You got some nerve. Don't tell me about Family Services. They don't service any family. I know all those guys. They never protected me, my mother, my sister—but you're gonna book me. My sister was never happier. I'm her brother. I think I know her a little bit better than you guys. We were providing a service. She was smiling a lot . . . (*In a rage*) She is *not* retarded. She's a little slow, that's all. You people are the real criminals for never doing a thing to help us. You have no idea what it's like to live where we live. Go ahead and book me. You won't get far. I'm not eighteen yet. I know the score. Go ahead and book me. But I ain't no criminal. I'm an entrepreneur, and my sister was never happier.

⊱⊰

I auditioned for the role of Tom Sawyer in a regional production of Big River. *The theater shall remain nameless, but the words* Paper *and* Mill *are both involved. So the character of Tom Sawyer is a supporting part. He is comic relief, and he gets a solo to sing called "Hand for the Hog." The song is all about his love of the swine. His hog is his best friend, his true companion. He would do anything for his hog. Et cetera. Bottom line: He loves pigs.*

Naturally, the director wanted to hear me sing the song, and, being the young professional I was, I was naturally prepared to do so. Now, the song contained a small musical interlude in the middle, and I thought I would prepare a little "dance" to fill the space. A small country western-themed jig, if you will.

Well, I get to this place in the music, and I begin my dance. It doesn't seem to have the effect I imagined it having while rehearsing it in my bathroom, so I decide to improvise a bit and throw in a few ad-libs. I shouted out (in time with the music, mind you) a simple "Oink! Oink!"

I don't know what didn't stop me there, but the next ad-lib was a high-pitched "Bacon!"

Bacon? The next thing that flew into my head was . . . bacon*? I decided to do a choreographed paddle turn so that I wouldn't have to look at the director's face. As I completed the turn and faced them again, I noticed that everyone was in a state of "slack jaw." I finished the song and received my polite "thank you" and left the room.*

I will have it known that two months later I was cast in George C. Wolfe's revival of On the Town, *which gave me my Equity Card and my big break. It was a chance I never would have gotten if I had gotten the role of Tom Sawyer at that nameless and rather important regional theater.*

Is the moral of this story "Everything happens for a reason," or does it serve another purpose? I ask this because even to this day I use the experience as a sort of "Barometer of Failure." After a bad audition, I ask myself, "Was it just bad, or was it bacon *bad?" Things are rarely* bacon *bad.*

—JESSE TYLER FERGUSON
ACTOR

Corporate Dress

AFRICAN AMERICAN MAN

You don't like the way I dress. That bothers you? I don't look corporate enough? Well, who says I want to look corporate? Who says every corporation won't like my style? The world is changing faster than you are. You're talking to me. That's a switch, right? Since when does a guy like you sit down with a guy like me and chat? So, you're here to advise me on my presentation? Look at you, all prepped and ready to go, and you think I should dress like you? Well, maybe I think other than that, no offense. The world keeps changing, so why don't you change your clothes? You sit there in that old khaki plaid get-up telling me what to wear to "win the job." I'm not winning anything, man. I work hard. They get me, they win. If they want me, they can take me in the box I'm wrapped in. They can give me some cash to buy me even a bigger, better wrapper. But till then . . . Sir, what exactly is the job that you have? Your position. What's it called? Senior Corporate Candidate Advisor for Minority Presentations. What does that mean exactly? All you have been advising me about is what to wear. Is that what your job is? Glorified fashion consultant? I'll be receiving my MBA in June, so let's go. I'm ready for some kind of real information here, but, so far, the only thing I know is that you don't like what I wear on my head and you don't like my shoes. It's not that I'm totally ungrateful for these tips on style. That Half-Windsor knot looks really dashing on you, but the whole tie thing doesn't fly with me. I guess there's something about having a loop around the throat that's a little reminiscent of something. They said this was a service for people like me to get ahead. A jump. Tell me, are you really a corporate worker, or do you just dress like one? Am I not being sufficiently grateful for being told that I look too much like a gangsta to succeed in the corporate world? Well, isn't that what you're sayin'? That's what it sounds like you're sayin' to me. How come the only thing you care about is what I'm wearing? Is this your mission, to be kind of a White Eye for the Black Guy?

How about a black eye from the black guy, huh? How's that sound? Don't panic, man. Don't get all sweaty and ruin your nice crisp shirt. Chill. If I were going to beat the crap out of you, I wouldn't precede it with a pun.

The Easy Rider

MATURE MAN

Oh, man, it was sweet! Weren't those choppers beauties? Those road sequences were so trippy. Dennis and Peter were stoned the whole time. We all were. It was a miracle of a film, man. Who knew it would be some cultural icon thing? See, those were the days, man! Little this, little that. Production, man. It was sweet! Set up sound, drive the trucks—whatever the moment needed, ya dig what I'm saying? That's the thing, man. It was all free-flowing, spontaneous. Did I ever tell ya about the time we were tripping? Walking down the Canyon just trippin' our faces off and—no joke—it was me, Dennis, and freakin' John Lennon. John Lennon, man! Shi . . . That was when L.A. was so freakin' real, man, not like now, some big freakin' mall. Listen, good for you, man. Ya got the whole house-and-pool thing going, but . . . Ya gotta get the indie thing going, man. That's the way to go. The whole TV thing, man, it's crap. Even when it's good, it's crap. Hey, did I ever tell ya about the time I was in Santa Cruz with Peter, looking for some location thing or something? We meet these two smoking chicks. We all get high in some gas station bathroom, go back to their place, have a total swap-meet, man—all of us—and then we find out one of them is, like, Clark Gable's illegitimate daughter, and we were, like, whoa! Gable, man! I told ya that story? Huh. Well, it's amazing, right? Gable, man! But ya see, that's what I'm talking about, man! We were in a zone, man—a total, creative, real zone. All I'm saying is that ya gotta get out there, man. Make your own deals. That's what Dennis and Peter did, man. They didn't listen to some studio. Go to Mexico for a year, get arrested, fall in love with some West Indian broad who cuts your heart out. Ya gotta live, man. Fall off that freakin' mountain. Hey, did I ever tell ya about the time Dennis and I got lost in Yellowstone freakin' Park? Man, we were so high. We were hallucinating polar bears in the middle of the summer. It was so freakin' real, man. See, *that's* what I'm talking about! Reality, man. Reality is, like, a totally . . . real thing, man.

The Father

MAN

Mutual funds, yeah. They really took off in the 90s, and I gotta say it's been a good business for me. I work downtown, but, you know, if you leave early enough you can miss all the traffic. I make it in, like, thirty-five, forty minutes. Not bad. My company has its own parking garage, so . . . Anyway, I'm doing all right, but, y'know, I'm . . . I feel bad for my wife. She's really gone through it—physically, mentally. She's kinda a wreck. Not sleeping. Lost her appetite. Me? I can sleep through an earthquake. And forget eating. I mean, you can see I haven't lost my appetite. So, you know, it's been hard on her. Her sister just had her second child six months ago, not even planned. It's something, right? We almost made it this time. Seven months. It's like God just doesn't want my wife to carry a baby full-term. Three. Three miscarriages. I gotta say I'm not the most religious guy, but I've been doing a lot of praying. It doesn't seem to be working. Then I get to thinking, like, maybe that time I cheated on the algebra regents is coming back to haunt me or something. Crazy, huh? But, hey, I'm not the one going through all this. I'm fine really. I go to work. I play basketball with my brothers. Yeah, we play at the Y—East Side. We get a family rate. It's great. The kids come and all. My sister-in-law is always taking yoga classes. My brothers all have kids. It's great, y'know? We're a big family. Six nieces and nephews already, and on my wife's side we got two. Do you have kids? Two, huh? Good for you. My wife said you were really nice to her. My feelings? My feelings are . . . This totally sucks. I mean, you get married, you think, "Easiest thing in the world. We'll get a house, couple of kids, the whole shebang, and that's it." But sometimes it's not so easy. There's this guy at work. His wife just had their first child—a girl. Y'know what he says to me? He was pissed. He said he always wanted his first child to be a boy and his second kid to be a girl. He was serious. What a freakin' asshole, right? I just walked away. It's a good thing I don't deal with him too much. What a jerk. We were having a girl. She was due in December. I was really excited because, honestly, Doc, Christmas is my absolute favorite time of year. Ask anyone that knows me. I'm, like, nutty about it. I don't know why exactly. I just have always loved the whole thing, even when I found out there was no Santa Claus. I didn't care. It was like, "It's still Christmas!" You should see my house. I make it into a winter wonderland. The neighbors love it. All the kids come over and look at all the lights and decorations and stuff. This year was gonna be extra special. I was thinking of the name Holly-Grace. Good for a December baby, right? Holly for the holiday and Grace 'cos she was our blessing. We were so close this time. So close. Sometimes I just don't know if I can go through this again. I don't mean to cry. It just really sucks, that's all. I'm kinda at a loss here. I don't know what we should do next. I just never thought becoming a father would be so hard. I hear people talking about how hard parenting is, and I keep thinking, "Hard?" For me, it would be so easy. So easy. Just give us the kid. We'll do all the rest. Holly-Grace. It's a good name, isn't it?

Forty—Hey!!!

MAN

Suggestion: This monologue can be acted using any comic accent, but Eastern European works particularly well.

Small leak, Mrs. Shapiro. I seal with tape for you today. I come back not tomorrow but day after. Tomorrow? My birthday. Wife. Big family celebration. Forty years old. Used to be, forty—hey!!! But now, forty, you're old. You turn on TV, everyone young. I see reality shows. Everyone teenager. At night, my wife and I see that David Letterman show, and I think, "If I am forty, he must be a hundred, no?" I know other plumber from building down block. He tell me he put Botox on forehead. You know Botox, Mrs. Shapiro? To make him younger. I say, "Victor, you are plumber. Why you do that?" He say, "Even plumber has to look good now." Everyone image-conscious. My wife think maybe he's gay, but I say, "No, he's a plumber." Do you believe this? What you think, Mrs. Shapiro? Would you put the Botox in your face? In my country, nobody image-conscious. Too busy working. I don't miss it, but America—crazy place, no? My father, he is eighty-five. Still strong as ox. So, for me, forty is young. No Botox for me. Tomorrow, I no work. I drink beer, I eat pierogi, I have cigar, I dance with my wife, I feel like young man. Forty—hey!!! You have good day, Mrs. Shapiro. Come day after birthday, I come with new pipe and fix your sink. No problem. Be like brand new. My pleasure, Mrs. Shapiro. My pleasure.

I love doing commercials! Some actors loathe doing and/or auditioning for them. Maybe I'm lucky in that I am a character actor and most of the auditions I get are to play "out-of-the-ordinary" kinds of guys. Even when I get an "average Joe"–type audition, it's usually great fun. I find that there is great camaraderie among my fellow commercial actors. Of course we all want the gig, but at a callback almost everyone realizes that, although you obviously gave a good audition to get called back, the ultimate decision about whom to cast often comes down quite simply to a "look."

—JOHN KUDAN
ACTOR, TWO HUNDRED COMMERCIALS

Georgia Red Clay

MATURE AFRICAN AMERICAN MAN

My daughter said you might be comin'. She's kinda worked up about this. She's been tryin' to get me to leave this place for years now, talkin' about the neighborhood being run-down and all and the house needing fixin'. You know how it is. Wants me to live with her in Virginia. But I always tell her, "Virginia's too north for me." Wouldn't you agree? Yeah, the house ain't fancy, but it's comfortable. Sure, look around. See, I've been living here for going on forty years. Lotta memories. Some things just can't be put into a photo album. You know what I mean. My family's been in Georgia a long time. Part of the slave trade. What's that saying? "Slave blood paved the way for Georgia Red Clay." Might be crazy, but I can't leave here. It's in my blood. You know how it is. See that tree? My granddaddy used to help push me up that tree so I could pretend I was an explorer. I got to be a mighty good climber, and thank the Lord I did 'cos gangs of white boys used to come through here and just beat us up with tire chains. Just for fun. They never got me, though. I was too fast for 'em. But my best friend, Malcolm, he was beat to death. I saw the whole thing from that tree. And right out this kitchen window, my mama used to sell pies. She baked the best pies this side of the Mississippi: apple pie, rhubarb pie, molasses pie, and—when they were just right—peach pie. Lordy, people loved my mama's pies. Right outside this window. I remember it like it was yesterday. You know what I'm saying? I got married right in this here backyard. Dogwoods were in full bloom—two pink, two white. You never seen anything so pretty, except Ida my wife. You folks married? Well, you know how it is then, don't ya? Have you been through the town? Up the street? Yup, the old button factory. Oh, it's been closed down now for years. I heard some rich fella from somewhere up north bought it and is gonna make it into deluxe apartments or something, but, man, I just love walking by it. You know, I worked there for thirty-five years. That's right. Night foreman for fifteen. Lotta struggle went on in that building. I always tell my daughter we made more than buttons in that place, you know what I'm saying? I worked the line with a lot good guys—Eddie Taylor, Curtis Moore, Sam Johnson. They all lived around here. Never forget the day an organizer came 'round and, boy, did he get Eddie all worked up. We found out they was cheatin' us outta overtime. Not the white guys. Just us. We wanted a union, and that was the end of it. Well, one day all hell broke loose. People fighting right there on the factory floor. They closed the place down for three full days, and we was all docked. They fired Eddie. Never worked another day in his life. Just lived with his mama and took to drink. Sad, real sad. Me and Curtis, we held on, and we eventually got that union. Tough days. You know how it is. Some things a daughter can't understand. You mean Jones' Funeral Home? Yeah, it's still there. It's where we black folk have all our funerals. I've been to all of them—my mama, my brother, Malcolm's, Reverend Wilkins, Mrs. Taylor. I've been to so many of 'em, I've lost count. But I knew 'em all, and they knew me. You know what I mean. Well, gentlemen, it's been nice spending this time with you, and I thank you for coming out and all, but, once again, we'll just leave it at that. Oh, I know my daughter's gonna be fightin' mad that I didn't accept your offer. She's always saying we took too little for too long, and she's right, of course, but, well, I'm just happy stayin' put is all. You know. Never was much of a firebrand, knockin' down walls with big sticks. I like to take things down one brick at a time, you understand. Well, gentlemen, have a good evening. I'm just gonna sit back and watch the sun go down. It's a lovely sight, wouldn't you agree?

Give a Mouse a Cookie

MAN
Suggestion: This monologue can also be played by a woman.

I have to go back to bed, Joel. You can't wake me up just to ask me questions you can ask me in the morning. I'm tired. I'm beat. I lie down, I toss and turn—and roll over—and just when I'm all relaxed and cozy in my own little stream of drool, you shake me awake and ask me a stupid question about nothing. Well, nothing important to me, okay? What you find important and what I find important at three A.M. is totally different. I can't believe you want to ask me all these questions—ever—but that they can't wait till tomorrow is crazy. I don't mind talking about politics, but not now. And I certainly don't want to have a debate about candidates. Who the hell cares who wins the election? No, I don't mean that really. I just don't care right at this moment about anything that doesn't concern me. I am selfish. I want to be selfish so much, but you keep interrupting me. The world could blow up for all I care. I want to close my eyes and pass out till seven fifteen when my alarm wakes me and I hear you snoring like a horse. That's unfair. You don't snore. You have a loud, continuous, self-satisfied snort. My whole morning routine is underscored with your nasal serenade. I don't mean to be mean. You are my houseguest, and I do want you to make yourself at home. The cookies are in the bottom drawer in the pantry, and the beer's in the fridge. Knock yourself out. I mean it. Good night.

Go Change

MAN

Suggestion: This character is intended to be a lighthearted, playful guy who cracks himself up with his gaffes.

Barbara! Barbara! C'mon, he'll be here in a few minutes. You don't wanna keep this one waiting. Look at you. You are so gorgeous. Your face, your hair. But . . . But you are not gonna wear that, are you? That dress. Well, that's just not a first-date dress. It's kinda like a "here-I-am, check-'em-out, help-yourself-to-these" dress! I did not say "cheap." I did not say "cheap." I didn't even imply "cheap." I'm sorry. I meant to imply "desperate." Just leave a little for the imagination, darling. What's left to imagine, you with clothes on? That thing is soooooo short. When ya turn around, you can see your whole Lopez hanging out. I'm sorry. I'm sorry. I shouldn't have made that crack about your ass. You know I think that your ass is fabulous. I worship it. If I weren't your brother, I'd hop it right now. But I am. So I won't. Go change. He can wait!

The Grown-Up

MAN

Yeah, that's my picture. Lotta good it's gonna do me now. So let me guess. You're a court-appointed shrink that my lawyer hired that is somehow gonna try to figure out a way for everyone to feel sorry for me. That actually I'm basically a good person who got mixed up with a bad crowd. Isn't that what you're doing here? Huh? I really am a sensitive artist type that unfortunately had a string of bad luck and made a few bad choices. Some tough breaks. Save yourself a lot of work, 'cos I'm gonna give it to you straight. I got hooked on smack, and that was the end of me. The end of my acting career, my marriage, the whole shebang. The only work I could get was crime. But for once in my life I'm not gonna let anyone else take the credit for my mess. Not my dad, my ex, my agent—not even my freakin' dealer. For once in my life I'm gonna be a grown-up, and I'm gonna take the rap. I was high, I broke in, stole the car, and, yes, I was holding a gun. There it is. The truth. So let's not sit here and strategize my plea. For once, I'm gonna take the rap. Seven years? I can live with it. And when I get out, I'm gonna start all over. Maybe I'll even act again. I'll get some good character parts, right? I can certainly say I lived it.

⊱⊰

Don't forget to play, don't forget to have fun, and don't forget to breathe.

If you have forgotten those three things and you're in the room and they've just said "let's see the scene" and you feel completely disconnected from all the things you've worked on and prepared and instead are trying to fit yourself into what you think "they" want, stop. Pick three things to get you in your body. Three things, like brushing your hand through your hair, pressing your right foot into the ground, and touching your index finger to a button on your chest. Three things that "they" probably wouldn't notice as something out of the ordinary but which momentarily ground you and allow you to then do your work. Ideally, decide on the three things before you enter the room.

Then after *the audition, even if you think you were atrocious, pick three things to praise. For instance, "I didn't push, I took direction, and I didn't throw up and run out of the room screaming." Again, anything. Give yourself credit. Be on your side. And then go buy yourself a treat. A latte, a lottery ticket, a lhasa apso. Gift yourself. Auditions can be tough.*

—DAN BUTLER
ACTOR/WRITER

Heart Assault

MAN

I've never been in love like this, or maybe I've never been in love at all until this. But my, Esther, you're all I can think about. I can't concentrate on anything in my life other than you. Oh, you take my breath away—for real. I had to get an inhaler from the doctor. I hyperventilate sometimes at work when I get a picture of you in my head. Honest, my heart is about to burst with feeling, but it's more like a heart attack. It's so big and powerful and intense. It's landed in my chest like a bomb about to explode. There's a hard mass in there. Seriously, feel it. No, don't. If you touch me, I know I'll pass out. Isn't love supposed to be kind to the heart? So why am I racked with pain? It's awful. Awful! I don't enjoy anything anymore at all. I can't escape it, either. You occupy my every thought. I can't get away from you, ever. It's like I'm being stalked. You stalk my thoughts. I love you so much my insides feel like they're going to burst out of me and splat on the wall behind your head, which isn't going to be good for either of us. So, I hope you understand, my darling Esther, I love you so much I've got to break up with you.

Impulse

MAN
Suggestion: This monologue can also be played by a woman.

I'm serious. I'm having a problem. I have to control these urges all the time. All I can say is it is a good thing nobody can tell, because I scare myself. It is all I can do to stop myself from doing what is in my head. I'm exhausted. I can lose it. I don't know if I can hold out. I never know *when*, either—when these impulses will strike, like an impulse to push some poor, unsuspecting person onto the subway tracks. Just looking at their trusting, oblivious faces makes me want to give a quick shove or a little kick with my leg just as the train is pulling into the station. Of course, I don't do it, but stopping myself is draining. And what if one day I don't stop myself? There is no reason for me to believe that I will be able to control myself in the future. I mean, it isn't always something dangerous. Sometimes it's just pushing someone's head into their ice cream. Or pulling some lady's skirt up. Or strapless top down. Or stepping on the dragging belt from someone's coat so they lose it and don't know it until a hundred people have walked over it. Cruel fantasies. Mean tricks! Tripping waiters, especially ones with full trays. Popping kids' balloons at Disney World. How great would that be? See, the possibilities are endless. It exhilarates me, and it's scary as hell. It's making me sick. Sometimes I think it is more painful to contain it. I should just do it. Let it out. And own up to it. Accept the consequences. Go to Hell. Burn for eternity. I have them more and more often. Don't laugh. Right now I am having one of those impulses. To spit in your coffee. Fart in your cushion. Bite your dog. See what I mean? So far I've only done one. Sorry.

Just My Style

MAN

So I've been caught red-handed, you say. Red-handed. What does that mean, exactly? Red-handed. Red as in blood, I bet. Bloody-handed. What else could it mean, actually? Sunburn? Communist? Nah. Bloody is definitely what it is. You should look that up. Anyway, I'm sorry. You caught me. I admit it. But not really red-handed. I was just borrowing some stuff, so I could look like someone substantial. Like I'm a person of substance. You know, like you. I want to look like you. Believe it or not, you're sort of my idol. I'm not being sarcastic. I really want to look like you do, with all your nice stuff. So somehow people might think I'm a person who can take care of myself, pay my bills, and have a life—like you. An interesting, successful life. A meaningful life. It may be a lie now, but maybe if I lie enough I can become my lie. And it won't be a lie anymore. It works. I've done it before. I know how this goes. If I don't buy it, who will? You did. So be cool. I trust you will. Why do you think I hang with you, man? Because I like you? I mean, I do like you. I admire you more than you could know. I emulate you. I practice you, practice being just like you. Haven't you noticed how much I've gotten like you? Look at you. Now look at me in your suit. Don't I look familiar? Well, this is how you look to other people. Pretty impressive, right? Confident, cool. I just don't know if there's room for both of us, though. Do you think there is room for the both of us? The jury is still out on that. We sure dress well. And I don't know about you, but I have a lot of cash in my wallet now, thanks to you. Do you need some? Probably, because I pretty much drained the account. Here, take something. It is the least I can do. I owe it all to you, guy. If it weren't for you, I wouldn't have anything, and now I am realized. Thanks, pal. And don't try to get away, okay? If you have me followed, you can say good-bye to someone you really care about. And I don't like to hurt little children any more than you do. Well, maybe a little more than you do. I don't mean to brag. At any rate, we both appreciate a good suit, so let's not get it dirty, okay? You don't really want to catch me red-handed. Believe that.

Let Him Sleep

MAN

Suggestion: This monologue can also be played by a woman.

Darling, look at him sleep. Look at him—so sweet, in his little bed, on his wee little pillow, thinking wee little thoughts. Do you think he'll be anything special—like us? We're special. We're amazing. He will be, too. He'll be more amazing than us, because we'll make sure of it. We should establish connections for him now, so he can move through life connected. Not like ordinary Joes, struggling so hard to get ahead, climbing up the ladder step by step. We must make sure he doesn't have to work so hard. But, that might not be good. He could become some little entitled brat, thinking the whole world owes him something, whining through life, demanding everything from everyone, expecting us to just pave the way. Let him make it on his own. We had to. It's better for his character. He'll appreciate life more. He should fend for himself. Have chores—hard ones—early on. Get up extra early, walk to school—no matter how far—in bad weather, do his share, earn his keep, toe the line, come up to the plate, for crying out loud. Sshhh—let's let him sleep. He has some hard work ahead of him. Or, shall we wake him up and let him get started? He's so lucky to have us. We are amazing. Good night, baby boy.

I love and respect actors and truly hope every auditioner does well. I've witnessed all of the following in auditions and hope these little suggestions will be of help to you. So . . .

Please don't approach the table uninvited, shake hands with everyone, and then *inform us that you have a cold. All we'll be thinking about while you sing is when we can go wash our hands.*

Please don't walk around the room, clapping your hands in the air, trying to find the best possible acoustical position from which to sing. And don't complain that the piano is out of tune. Deal with it.

Please don't snub the piano player or give him or her a dirty look when your pages go all over the floor because they're not fastened properly. Playing pianos while turning pages is hard enough. And please don't hand over a sheaf of old, crumpled, weary music and ask them to transpose on the spot. Greet them when you enter. Thank them when you leave. This is your colleague.

Please *don't wear a costume. You can give a hint of character, but don't bring your top hat and spats.*

Please don't bring props unless they are absolutely necessary for your audition. One actor memorably pulled out a large kitchen knife and wielded it in our faces as he sang. Had there been a red button marked "Security" beneath the table, it would have been pushed. As it was, the actor's agent was immediately called, and we've never seen this actor again. He may be in Sing Sing for all I know, the place where singing actors go who use props.

Please don't move forward as you sing until you're a foot away, staring directly into our eyes and emoting "just for us." It makes us very, very uncomfortable. Keep your distance. Focus somewhere and sing for *us, not* to *us. And please don't ask us to sing along, clap, or participate in any way. I don't want to have to laugh and smile cheerily as you tell me "my feet's too big."*

Please don't chew gum. Take it out before you come in. Don't stick it on the piano or behind your ear.

Understand that, usually, your reputation precedes you. The people behind the table will always try to find out in advance of hiring you whether you are "trouble backstage," miss shows, are a diva, have an attitude, are obnoxious or unpredictable onstage, or have any other problems we should know about. Theatre requires a group dynamic of collaboration, consistency, and kindness, and we do our best to avoid problematic people. If it's between you and someone equally talented, we'll always take the person with the better rep. Life is short, and theatre is hard.

—LYNN AHRENS
TONY AWARD–WINNING COMPOSER/WRITER

Madeline

YOUNG MAN

Look at that. What a set of cans! Look, man. Wouldn't ya love to give her a ride on the ol' bone rollercoaster? You missed it. Look, she's turning around. Hurry up. Yeah, she wants it. She wants to do the no-pants dance. Why aren't you looking? You're missing them all today. That isn't healthy. There's some premium tail going by, and you, you got to look. I'm starting to feel like I'm alone here. You got to see it, too, or it isn't the same. What's up with you? I know what's up with me. The usual. Hey, why aren't you with me here? Shit, you aren't thinking about *her* are you? I swear that's all you do now. She isn't worth it. C'mon, how whipped are you? There is so much out here, man. We should be making plans to occupy Vagistan. I am too horny for one chick. I'm so horny I could hump a dump truck. Maybe I will. Now you're getting all content with some cow. Madeline was a hook-up. Now you're, like, attached to her. Stop it. I don't like it. It sucks. She'll start demanding your complete, one-hundred-percent attention and get possessive and jealous. That's how they get. And what about me, huh? What about us? We're a team, you and me. We have fun. We don't want her getting in the way. We keep it light, right? Don't we? Well, shit, why don't you answer me?! Are you even listening? You don't even answer me anymore. It's all "Madeline, Madeline." I have an idea. Why don't you go call Madeline, your little girlfriend, if that's what you want to do. Go ahead. See if I freakin' care. I don't need you. I don't care what you do. See that chick every day if you want to. I don't care if you see her every minute. I hope you do. Just go, okay? Just go.

Miss Horace

YOUNG MAN

Please don't fire me, Mr. Shultz. Please don't fire me. And please forgive me, Miss Horace. I didn't mean to offend anyone, I assure you. I just think Miss Horace here has a nice smile, and I told her. I'm ever so sorry, Miss Horace. I meant no harm. No, I didn't know that was suggestive. The comment, sir? About what? Her lips? Well, that was just an extension of the compliment about her lovely smile, and for that I am sorry, Miss Horace, if I have offended you in any way. Yes, I did say something about her not needing to wear anything else but her smile. But I . . . But I . . . But I meant, sir—I was referring to how . . .Yes, sir. I wink at *everyone*, sir. It's not flirtatious at all. It's not a come-on kind of wink. It's more of a blink, actually. A tick. Kind of a spasm. I was born with it. A sort of seizure. I converted it to be socially acceptable. I take medication for it, sir. Really. I'll remember to take it. Yes. Thank you, Mr. Shultz. I appreciate the warning. And for understanding. And good day to you, Miss Horace. Have a nice day. And, once again, my humble apology. (*She exits*) I can't believe I offended Judy. No, I always call her that. Or "Torpedo Tits." Sorry. Oh, come on. Do you really call her Miss Horace? It's just that no one does. She's pretty friendly, if you know what I mean. I know you have a lot of meetings at night, sir, but—well, you should hang with us sometime after work. She is a party girl, that Judy. She is total fun. No, that is no reason for anyone to forget themselves in the workplace. But, just man to man, you have to admit Judy—Miss Horace—is way hot and must run into trouble wherever she takes that luscious bootay of hers. And her lips are famous, if you know what I'm saying. Ask anyone. Everyone in the place is banana pants for her. She loves it. She isn't here, so we can talk man to man for a sec, right? No, I did not know you were engaged to her. Wow. Really? Congratulations! Good going! Well, what can I say? She is—I mean, with all due respect, sir, from one guy to another . . . Are you going to fire me, Mr. Schultz?

No More

YOUNG MAN

No thanks, I don't want a hit. I haven't changed, man. I just don't feel like smoking, okay? It makes me feel weird. I'm not stopping you, so what's the problem? I'm just tired of it all. You know, hanging out. I realize kinda—I don't know. Yes, I do. Okay, I realize sometimes that I don't want to hang with you anymore. It isn't you, man. I don't want to just be hanging all the time. I want to do something. I want to go somewhere. I don't mean the mall, genius. Somewhere, you know, in the future. The future better be better than now, 'cause this sucks. Can't you see it? We're losers. I don't want to end up like Rolondo. I know we're not him, but what happened to him taught me something. Didn't it teach you anything? We can't keep this up, with the smoke and the hanging and the nothing. For what? It isn't even fun anymore. It doesn't take us anywhere. The high feels bad. I think bad thoughts, like I'm just standing still and time goes by without us in it. I don't know how to say it, but we just get stupid. I don't mean to call you stupid, but look at us, blowing smoke up each other's noses. Look at us. Look at us, man. We look horrible, like a couple of zombies or something, like we don't care. And I do kind of care. The only people who think we're doing fine are the guys we hang with, like Terry and Pete. And Terry's okay, but Pete looks like ass. We're losers. Don't you see it? All of us, okay? I'm not dissing just you. I'm not. I'm dissing me, too. I know I gotta do something soon. Here's the bus. I'm heading back. I don't know. Maybe I'll try out for baseball. I can throw a ball. You can throw a ball. We used to do it all the time. What do you think? There's tryouts today. What do you say, man? You coming?

Not Lonely

MATURE MAN

Census survey? Well, young man, don't tell the IRS it's only me in this big old house! And don't tell the widows in town, either. They call me up all the time as it is. Ya think I'm kidding? Lemme tell ya something. Everyone tells ya how horrible it is to get old. It's not getting old that's the problem; it's getting sick and dying that's the problem. And I'm not sick. I'm here to tell ya that getting older can be a hoot. For one thing, I do whatever the hell I want. I have bacon and eggs for breakfast every morning, followed by my cigar with a shot of whiskey. Wakes up the blood. And then I check my email, look at some porn, get excited, and then I take a nap. I get up whenever the hell I feel like it. Maybe I'll take a walk, maybe I'll make some calls, read the paper—whatever I want to do. Sometimes I call my lady friend and we see a movie, have some dinner, a little wine, a little canoodle, she's home by midnight. I'm telling you, it's the life of Riley. People think I'm lonely, but I'm not. My daughter, she's always calling. "Dad, you must be lonely. Come on over." I tell her, "I'm not lonely." And honestly, I only like one of my grandkids—Leah, my son's daughter. She's a living doll, but the rest—spoiled brats. You can have 'em! I love all the gossip shows. I don't know who they're talking about half the time—Paris this or Britney that—but whatever. They're all these trampy girls. I get a kick out of them. They all seem to be hopped up on something, and they constantly take their clothes off. I've never seen anything like it! I laugh my ass off! They didn't have shows like this when I was growing up, I'll tell ya that. See, if my wife was still around, I wouldn't be able to watch these shows. She wouldn't like it. Linda was a nice girl but a bit of a prude. I used to go elsewhere to get the fancy stuff, if you catch my drift. But we got along alright. She was a good girl, a good mother. I miss her. Not too often—just at certain times of the day. Late afternoons, usually, like on Sundays. That's a tough time. She cooked a lot of stuff on Sundays, for the week. The house smelled—well, it smelled good. Chicken vapors all over the place. Egg noodles boiling. Vanilla, 'cos she baked a lot. You know, comfort food. Comfort food is very comforting, no doubt about it. Every Sunday. (*Pause*) She died. It happens to all of us. She didn't deserve it. She went fast. Whatta ya gonna do? I'm okay. Still got all my teeth. Yeah, I'm not lonely. Just a little slower. People die. Whatta ya gonna do? (*Pause, looks at watch*) Oh, my show is on! Stick around. Ya gotta see this. These girls are a mess.

⊱⊰

It isn't about presenting yourself. It is about being yourself. It helps when you identify with the material. Then you can truly use yourself and make it personal. Don't act. Just be.

—ELISSA MYERS
CASTING DIRECTOR

Phobias

MAN
Suggestion: This monologue can also be played by a woman.

How can you judge how I'm feeling? For your information, my phobias are real. I'm a very phobic personality. I don't just decide to have a phobia when I need one. How insulting. You think I just develop this little condition when I don't feel like doing what you want me to do? You think it is just convenient for me to have a flare-up of agoraphobia because I don't want to go out and earn a living or visit Mother? Well, it isn't like that, I'll have you know. I have a genuine fear of going out of the house. It is an illness. You shouldn't make fun. Of course, I have to go out occasionally, you know, when it's urgent. I have to go to the dentist, rotate my tires, buy lottery tickets. I have not been to the beach. I got this tan through the window in the sun room, Colombo. If I don't put on sunscreen, I burn to a crisp in this house. You can't tell because today it is overcast in here. It's probably going to rain—another reason to stay in. I'm scared of the rain. I have a fear of melting. Don't laugh. It's sad. You have a lot of nerve, coming in here and accusing me of being a lazy good-for-nothing. You have to realize I have a lot of problems that I can't control. I'm fragile. I can't do things like other people. I have a panic disorder when I am made to do things I don't feel like doing. That is why I don't work, big shot. I panic. I panic a lot. There's plenty of reason to panic. I don't do well with bosses. They work me up. They're too—I don't know—they're too bossy. And I'd love to visit Mother, more than anything. I'm just not able to. I don't expect you to understand, but, when you see her, tell her I love her and she's late on my rent. I just want her to know because I don't want her to get charged a late fee. There is nothing wrong with her sending me money. She loves taking care of me. She knows how ill I am. She isn't a Doubting Thomas like you. It would be nice if she would come visit me. That would be nice. I love Mother. Mother can visit me anytime. I'd love it, as long as she takes her shoes off at the door and doesn't use my bathroom. That's not asking so much. She can go before she leaves her house, right? It isn't personal. She knows nobody pees in my bathroom, ever. It's my rule. It's my golden rule. Don't be mad at me. I can't help it. I'm very delicate. Be thankful that I'm still alive. Because, Buster Brown, there is nothing like family.

Plain and Simple

MAN

Sandy, honey, could you just not ask me so many questions about her? She shouldn't matter. Because she doesn't matter to me anymore. She only matters to you, which of course matters to me, Sandy, but isn't this whole thing ridiculous? We don't have to deal with her. At all. I don't talk to her. Never. Never, I swear to God. Not in two months. I promise. Okay, I said "Hello" when she passed us. I forgot. Wouldn't not saying "Hello" have been worse? Is that what you are counting as keeping in touch? Isn't that just common politeness? "Hello" is what you say to anyone, everyone. And that was how long ago? Alright, not that long ago, but she is a nonissue. Please, baby, I don't even remember the incident—hardly. And she didn't even look good. At all. Seriously, she was all made up like she was going to a ball at two in the afternoon. Ridiculous, if you ask me. She was all hair and heels and leather straps all over, strutting like she's on a runway in Paris, with everybody drooling all over her, which I wasn't. Other people maybe were. Are you kidding? She doesn't hold a candle to you. You don't even have to try. Your beauty is way better—modest and humble. I love how you are—plain and simple. I hate obvious beauty. Be happy your beauty isn't so apparent. I don't care about her. I don't even like the way she smells. Did you get a whiff? That lavender crap she slathers all over her skin—how could you miss it? I'm glad you're not so obsessed with yourself, moisturizing every pore of your body. I used to sit there watching her for hours, massaging emollients all over her body, just so she could glow. Who needs to glow? Would you tell me? You don't. I mean, you glow from the inside. That's even better. You should be happy people don't look at you that way. You kidding? She's the one who has a problem, not you. And certainly not me. I hardly remember her. She's all a blur. You know, Sandy, you think about her too much.

The Realist

MAN

Lemme tell ya, Ali, the studios did not like having her around. I was constantly running interference. I couldn't keep writing with her. It was just too much work. You know this is a business where's there's a lot of give and take. Your mom was never good at that. She was great at taking, but not giving. Alright, alright, I won't bad-mouth her, Ali, but really . . . Look, I know you and your brother got caught in the middle, and that was bad, I know. But what was I supposed to do? Sit home and play nursemaid to her? Somebody has to go out there and make a living—bring home the bucks. It's not my fault I was more successful on my own. Jesus, why do we have to rehash this? I can't change the past. I feel bad. I love you. Why can't we just take it from here? Let's deal with now. Jennifer does like you. It's just that she's not your mom, and she has her own career. Ali, we work our butts off. I'm in my office, like, fourteen hours a day. Something your mother has never done, I may add. Ali, please don't walk away. I'm sorry. Am I supposed to feel bad about being successful? Those bucks I make support you and your brother and those private schools that the two of you keep getting kicked out of. And don't start that again, Ali. You can't pin her drinking on me. She had problems way before our divorce. And by the way, who do you think paid for her rehab? Oh, honey, I don't want to fight anymore. How many times can I say I'm sorry? I wasn't the father you needed, and I am truly, truly sorry about that. Your mother's not in good shape, and I am very sorry about that as well. Life isn't perfect, Ali. That's why God invented therapists. (*Pause*) Are you back in school? Are you doing okay? Do you have enough friends? Ali, if you don't want to talk, I understand, but we can't keep going over and over this stuff. (*Looks at watch*) I gotta get back to the studio. I'm gonna be working till at least eleven. Look, I'll call you over the weekend. Maybe you and your brother can come over for dinner. You pick a day. I'll make sure I'm free, if that's what you want. Ali, I love you so much. I want to get past all this. (*Pause*) Lemme do this. Here's a check. Maybe it will help your mother a bit. If you need more, let me know. You have my cell phone number, right? Call me anytime after seven. If you don't get through, leave a message. I'll call you back as soon as I can. So listen, call me about dinner next week. I want this to happen, okay? Okay? I'll see you soon.

The Relic

MAN

Steve, don't get me started. Do *not* get me started. This is what I've been saying. We are now being bashed by our own people! When I see that pansy nephew of yours, I am going to give him a piece of my mind. This new generation. *Uh!* I have a mind to make him sit through the movie of *Mame* five times. This is the ultimate—gay people telling us we're *too* gay. Is that like being "too Black"? Or "too Danish"? Don't have that herring! "Too Danish!" Unbelievable. We marched in every parade for ten years so we could be "big old queens" and feel good about ourselves, and now we're "too gay" just because these missies all want to get legally married and have kids? I guess gay is the new straight. Makes me want to stay in the gay ghetto. At least our neighborhoods haven't lost any real estate. How long have we been out? Over fifteen years, right? Well, there is no going back to that closet now, I'll tell you. These straight-acting gays. *Please!* I worked hard to be fabulous, and I want to stay that way! We're old-fashioned, Steve. The old folk who still like musicals and good skin care. Although you know I always thought Cher was overrated, just for the record! *Ohmygod!* Did you see that recent picture of Barbara? Honey, she needs lipo, like . . . *yesterday!* Oh, you're a bitch. She still sings like a goddess! Oh, brother. Yep, out-and-out dinosaurs—that's us. Well, all these kids wanna be mainstream. I get it, I get it. I don't think it's much fun, but I get it. We're relics, Steve, but, hey, relics should be treasured, right? Oh, you're a bitch. Sit down. I'll do your highlights.

I don't like to know anything about the people I am auditioning for. I think of it like I am going to a party, to meet new people. I love it.

—MARGO MARTINDALE
ACTOR

Rodeo Stud

YOUNG MAN

Well, ma'am, I do rodeo. I ride bulls. I'm here 'cos my girlfriend saw this ad and sent in my picture and I got this call and, well, I came here. From Tennessee, ma'am. Oh, it is beautiful country. Yup, *Coal Miner's Daughter*. They filmed that not too far from where I'm from. My girlfriend's back there now taking care of the dogs. I got four of 'em. Pit bulls. I agree. They're misunderstood. My shirt? Sure, I can take it off. It's kinda hot in here, anyway. (*Takes off shirt*) Yes, ma'am, riding bulls definitely builds up a lot of muscles. Yeah, all over. Ya need to be strong to hold on to them animals. That's right, ma'am, rough and tumble. No, ma'am, these are the tightest jeans I have. Turn around? Sure. (*He turns around and now talks to his interviewer as he faces backward.*) Yup, ridin' bulls does make your thighs mighty strong. Turn sideways? Sure. So, is this a physically demanding film? 'Cos I think I'd be good at that. I love action. I guess rodeo must be in my genes, 'cos my daddy rode 'em, too. He even won a state championship once. That's my goal—state level. And then, who knows? Like I said, ma'am, these are the tightest jeans I have. Turn around? Oh, sure. (*Faces front*) A thousand dollars! Sure, who couldn't use a thousand dollars? I'm just wondering, what's the basic story of the movie? Country girl gets lost in the city? That sounds like a good story. Lemme guess. Then she meets her Prince Charming—*me*! And they live happily ever after! She meets a lot of Prince Charmings? I'd be one of them. Well okay! Pull these down a bit? Alright. (*Loosens jeans a little and pulls them down a bit*) This city is bigger than I thought. More spread out. I'll tell ya, one person I'd love to meet is Sandra Bullock. I love her. Have you worked with her? No, huh? So, I'm just wondering, do you need me to say some of the lines for you, so I'd be ready for the scenes? No lines? Well, okay then. Well, actions speak louder than words, right? Hey, I just got an idea. Since this girl meets all these guys, I could be the Rodeo Guy. Maybe I even meet her at a rodeo. I got all my rodeo clothes with me. Don't need 'em? Just the hat. Well, alright, I'll bring the hat! Wait till I tell my girlfriend that I really am gonna be in a movie. She'll be so excited. Thank you, ma'am. I'll be here, bright and early.

She's a Fake

MAN

I'm saying she's not insecure. "Insecure" is someone who will step back and try not to be noticed. She is so not that. She makes you feel that you have a say in everything, but she's fooling you. She acts all scared and shy, but she gets you to notice her that way. And gets you to think you are rescuing her. You can't save her, but you can save your time and money. Don't you see that she is getting you caught in her web? Oh, come on, really. Really. She asks you your opinion constantly, but she's forming your opinion. She's so modest and humble. "Do I really look okay?" She knows she looks good. Don't be fooled. You can't help her with her problems. She doesn't have any real problems. She has you running to her side, boosting her self-esteem. Bullshit. Vulnerable? There's not a vulnerable bone in her body. What advice does she need from you? What advice? "Do my boobs look too big in this dress?" is not a problem and cannot be a problem in anyone's book. There is no such thing as anyone's boobs being too big for anything. Anyone knows that. What is she asking? They enter a room a full minute before she does. How do you answer that? "Yes, they do"? "They really pop out of that dress." Wow, what a great problem. She's got you right where she wants you. The broad's a fraud. And, frankly, I think she likes me better.

Study Hall

YOUNG MAN

Do you want some chewing gum? I just wondered because I always need to chew when I study. I know it isn't allowed, but that makes it, well, more dangerous. Okay, never mind. I'll just get you in trouble. You're so good not to talk. I guess I just like to push the envelope. Live on the edge. I hear you might be joining math club. I think you should. My mom said it would be better to do sports, but she doesn't know how exciting problem solving can be. You want me to graph that parabola? Just let me know. I wouldn't mind. I'm doing it in my head anyway. We're having a pi party. At the club. The math club. You can come as my guest or whatever. It's a "Pi-R-Square Dance." It's dress up. You come in costume. I'm going as a rhombus. Unless you want to go as a rhombus. I could change. I could do a three-sixty and go as a circle. I have a math joke for every occasion. Yeah, I have a million of them. I don't only have a dark side, you know. Some people think mathematicians "have a covenant with the devil to darken the spirit and confine man in bonds of hell." St. Augustine said that as a warning to all good Christians. Don't be scared. I'm more fun than that. I keep it light. I have humor. I have to. You'd get destroyed around here without it. Last year I went to the party as Pythagoras. Of course, they called me Py*fag*oras. So what? I can take a joke. I'm safe with rhombus, don't you think? Don't you think? Just nod. Thank you. I like you. Would you think me "obtuse" if I told you that you were "acute" girl? What did the constipated mathematician do? He worked it out with a pencil. Sorry. Do you think he used a number two pencil? Sorry. Sorry if I went off on a tangent. Sometimes I don't think. Therefore, I am not. Do you know—do you know that you have a perfectly symmetrical face? I am being totally serious here. That is how beauty is measured in every culture in the world. You have perfect symmetry. That is the first thing I noticed about you. That and your parallel hair. Just nod your head if you will go to the dance with me. Yes? Snap! I'll bring my Rubik's Cube.

Useful

YOUNG MAN
Suggestion: Try a Midwestern accent.

Can I help you with anything, anything at all? I might not be much to look at, but I'm useful, at least. I like to do things with my own two hands. With my own two hands, Willing and Able. That's what I call them. I'm ambidextrous, you know. I'm equally efficient with either one. Maybe I'm a little stronger on the left, but I don't favor it. Especially during meals, if I'm seated next to a right-leaning supper partner. I try to be polite. There sure are a lot of bugs out here. Are you itchy? I am. I won't scratch it, because it isn't in a nice place. Like I said, I do have manners. Unless you happen to look away. Then I can do it real fast, but I probably won't. You have a cute laugh. I know you're shy. I like it. I do. People don't have to keep talking back a lot. It is fine to be quiet. Shy people are nice. They don't interrupt you. I like that. But being you're shy is why it's taking me so long to talk to you. I don't want to do it wrong and scare you. Scare you away because I know that you like me. I can tell that. It doesn't happen much, and when it does it usually is someone not so shy. Sometimes they're married and wanting something they shouldn't be having. I don't ever. No. I know I'm useful but not like that. But you, you, you're . . . wow, so sweet and nice, and I know you wait for me every day. I've noticed it for awhile. I just wanted to wait before I started up with you. Wait till I was sure it was me that you were waiting for. And now I know it was. I am right. Right? There's that cute laugh again. You really have a cute laugh. It says a lot about you, that laugh. It says that you have a funny bone and that you tickle easy. Do you tickle easy? Well, I guess so, is my guess. If I am lucky, I will find out how to tickle you. I think the bugs like it, too.

In the late '50s I went a few times as "an observer" to the Actors' Studio. On one occasion Anne Bancroft and Kevin McCarthy did a scene from My Fair Lady/Pygmalion, *and when they finished—before Strasberg gave this criticism—Kevin apologized for the roughness of the performance, saying, "I was really very nervous," and Strasberg said, "In theater there are many things that can go wrong. The set can fall down, someone in the audience can have a coughing fit or a stroke, you can have really bad headaches or a broken heart, your partner can forget the lines—anything can happen! The one thing you can depend on is that* you will always be nervous! *You cannot use that as an excuse for not fulfilling your performance. You must put the nerves into your preparation. You can't ignore them or suppress them. Use them." Wise advice! And, I promise you, not really all that much easier said than done.*

—RICHARD EASTON
TONY AWARD–WINNING ACTOR

Well Spent

MAN

Well, I told her—right out. I did. You think I don't speak my mind, but I do. I said . . . I said . . . you know, something like, "I know we spend a lot of time together, and a lot of the time together we spend a lot of money, and I've spent some time thinking about all the money we spend, and, well . . . sometimes we should spend more time not spending so much of my money." She didn't like the "my money" part. She said she thought we were closer than that. And I said, "We are close, and I'm sorry if I hurt you, but," I said, "maybe we could spend less of our money because we're running out of our money. And I have to pay some important bills." And she said we should decide together which bills are important—and some of those bills she shouldn't have to worry about. Which I agreed is only fair—that maybe she shouldn't have to worry about my bills. But, see, then I said, "Well, maybe my bills I should spend my money on, which is the money I was talking about not spending—previously." See, I told her sort of like that. She said she wasn't buying all my crap. I said, "If you could stop buying crap we wouldn't be in all this crap to begin with." And I laughed and said it was a joke. But she didn't think it was funny, which surprised me because she's really a fun girl. But she said that I was "indirectly cruel" and that she doesn't mind the cruel if it is directly so. So, I said that I try to be polite whenever possible and that direct cruelty does not show good manners. And she said, "Screw good manners," which I said is not the answer ever. She was not pleased. She said I owe her. I owe her a lot. I said, "Right now, I owe everybody a lot. Join the list." Then she slapped me—with a lawsuit, which is why I'm here. I need your advice. Please tell me, how do I get her back?

White-Collar

MAN

Look, Laura, I am begging you to help me through this trial. You're my wife, goddamn it, and I need my wife beside me! Of course I understand how humiliated you are. How do you think I felt being taken out of my office in handcuffs? You think I'm having a picnic here, a day in the park? They paraded me down the corridor like a fucking common criminal—for something I did not do! You still don't believe me, do you? Do you?! Do you think I would risk my entire business, my career for some stupid inside trade just because I wanted a million dollars? We have a million dollars, Laura! Listen, I'm begging you, you've got to believe me. I didn't know a goddamn thing. I am pleading not guilty because I'm innocent. These charges are never gonna stick. Jesus, I don't believe this. My lawyer believes me, but not my wife! I know I've done some messed up things in the past, but we've had a pretty damn great life because of what I do. Whatever you've wanted, you've gotten. Don't our kids have the best of everything? Huh? I've never denied you anything. Oh, for Christ's sake, Laura, don't start with that again. You know I haven't seen that woman in over a year. You're never gonna let me forget that, will you? Look, let's just get through this trial and then whatever, whatever you wanna do. We'll start over, we'll move, we'll travel. Whatever you wanna do. I will make this up to you, I promise. You think I'm going to jail! I'm not going to jail. I am not going to jail! This is unbelievable. My own wife. So that's it. Thirteen years down the tubes? Okay, you want to play hardball? Is that what you want? I'm a deal-maker. I'll make you a deal. You tell me what it's gonna take for you to stand by me. I'm all ears. And just think about this. What kind of message are you sending our kids, that you're gonna walk out on their father after he's begged you to stay? You might hate me, but they don't. So what's it gonna take, Laura? Huh? I got the checkbook out. What's it gonna take?

The Winking Jesus

MAN

Ma, no, I'm not hungry. Yeah, I know, I read it in the paper. That doesn't mean it's true, Ma. Remember a few years ago when someone saw the Blessed Virgin in a piece of cheese? It always happens in some neighborhood where there isn't even a subway stop. Nobody can ever witness it. Ma, ya can't believe those tabloids. Some cleaning guy says some Jesus statue opened his eye and winked at him? Maybe the cleaning guy is just crazy. Did anyone think of that? Now he's a celebrity. The cleaner, Ma, not Jesus. I know Jesus has been big for a long time now. I mean it, Ma. I'm not hungry. Don't you think it's weird that Jesus would pick some church stuck between a dry cleaner and an Italian ice outlet to perform a miracle *and* the miracle only turns out to be a wink? We could use bigger miracles than that. Like feeding starving children, or at least cure Uncle Mario's phlebitis. Ma, I'm not a cynic. I'm just a little more choosy in what I do believe in. Of course I believe in God. Yes, Ma, I'll try to go to church more. I'm just saying I don't think you should believe every little thing you see or hear just because it's in a paper or on some TV show. Like when you went on those psychic shows. They all told you the same thing about Dad. He's at peace, he loved you, and you might need an operation soon. What seventy-five-year-old person might not need an operation soon? You know you could talk directly to Dad all by yourself. You think TV personalities have a better connection? Lemme tell ya, Ma, the signal is particularly strong during sweeps week. Alright, whatever you want to believe, Ma. Ma, not now. Lasagna for breakfast is a little too heavy. I love your lasagna, Ma. I just don't want it for breakfast. (*Beat*) Alright, I'll have some. Just promise me you won't make a pilgrimage to see some winking Jesus.

You Do It Every Time

MAN

Suggestion: This monologue can also be played by a woman.

You do it every time. You never follow the rules. There *are* rules. Rules. It's a recipe. Someone worked it out, and look—it's published. It doesn't say, "Add onions." You did. It says, "Serve at room temperature." You've heated it up. It's supposed to be an appetizer. You've got it as a side dish. Side dish. It says, "Serve with a crisp white wine and a crusty bread." You have Chianti and corn muffins. It says shitake. You add morels. It never stops, ever. Don't you think there are reasons she made it so specific? Wouldn't she say, "Onions optional"? My God, it's like you're out of control. Why don't we just eat off the floor? You have it all at your fingertips. You're working on a Viking. Everything you have is top of the line, but it never ends with you. If it says, "Preheat oven," you put it in while it's cool. And I don't care if people think you're a good cook. The crew you invite over here, they just want free grub. They've obviously never eaten in the finer restaurants. Hold on. Don't throw that out. I was still eating it.

Quite often, it's a comfortable, confident audition that illuminates for the director what s/he is looking for. And by this, I mean those certain qualities which you alone possess. That being said, it follows that you therefore are never really in competition with anybody else who is auditioning for the same part. You alone are you, so be prepared and bring it to the table! And at the end of it, an audition is a business transaction. You're selling, and they're buying. If they're not interested in your wares, try not to take it personally. Soon enough there will be another buyer who will snap up your entire inventory!

—CARL ANDRESS
DIRECTOR/AUTHOR

Performance Rights

Donna Daley and Julie Halston
c/o Heinemann
361 Hanover Street
Portsmouth, NH 03801–3912

About the Authors

Donna Daley has worked extensively as actress and is coauthor of *Mama Drama* (Samuel French), originally produced Off-Broadway at the Ensemble Studio Theatre and the Cleveland Play House, where she created the role of Lizzie. She is the author of "Sandi's Agreement" in *Best Scenes for the 90s* (Applause Theatre and Cinema Books). She developed and directed *Beat: A Subway Cop's Comedy*, which had an eight-month Off-Broadway run and which was developed into a sitcom for UPN. She was a cofounding member of the CNL Collective under the auspices of Women's Interart, where she wrote, developed, and acted in numerous plays. Her play *The Misconception of Iggy* was presented at Polaris North, MCC and The Actor's Studio with Anne Meara. She developed and directed the NYC production of Stephanie Musnick's one-woman show *A Saint for All Wash Cycles*. She was a contributing writer and created voices for such animated series as *Sky Dancers* and *Dragon Flyz* on ABC, *Vanpires* on FOX, and *Happiness: The Secret of The Loch*, which were the recipients of the Dove Foundation Award, the Family Circle Choice Award, and the Video Humanitarian Award, respectively. Miss Daley was a 2004 Writer in Residence at the New Harmony Project with her play *Deeply Shallow*. She lives in New York City, where she coaches and writes tailor-made monologues for individual actors. She and Miss Halston have collaborated on several projects including the animated short "Open Call" and a new book for young people.

Julie Halston is one of today's busiest actresses. Well known to theatre audiences, she has appeared in numerous Broadway and Off-Broadway shows, including *Hairspray, Gypsy, Twentieth Century, The Women,* and *The Vagina Monologues*. A founding member of Charles Busch's now-legendary company Theatre-in-Limbo, she costarred with Mr. Busch in many of their productions, including *Vampire Lesbians of Sodom, The Lady in Question,* and *Red Scare on Sunset*. She wrote and starred in her own critically acclaimed show, *Julie Halston's Lifetime of Comedy*, which led to a CBS development deal. Miss Halston has been the recipient of many award nominations, including the Drama Desk, The Outer Critic's Circle, and The Drama League. Television audiences have seen her as Tina Carmello on the CBS comedy *The Class* and Bitsy Von Muffling on *Sex and the City*. Like many a New York actor, she can be seen on a number of episodes of *Law & Order*. Her films include *I Think I Love My Wife, The Juror, Small-Time Crooks, Addams*

Family Values, and *A Very Serious Person*, which is shown regularly on Showtime. Miss Halston has collaborated with Miss Daley on a number of projects including the animated short "Open Call" and currently on a book for young people. www.juliehalston.com